A Contemporary Perspective
GWR Signalling

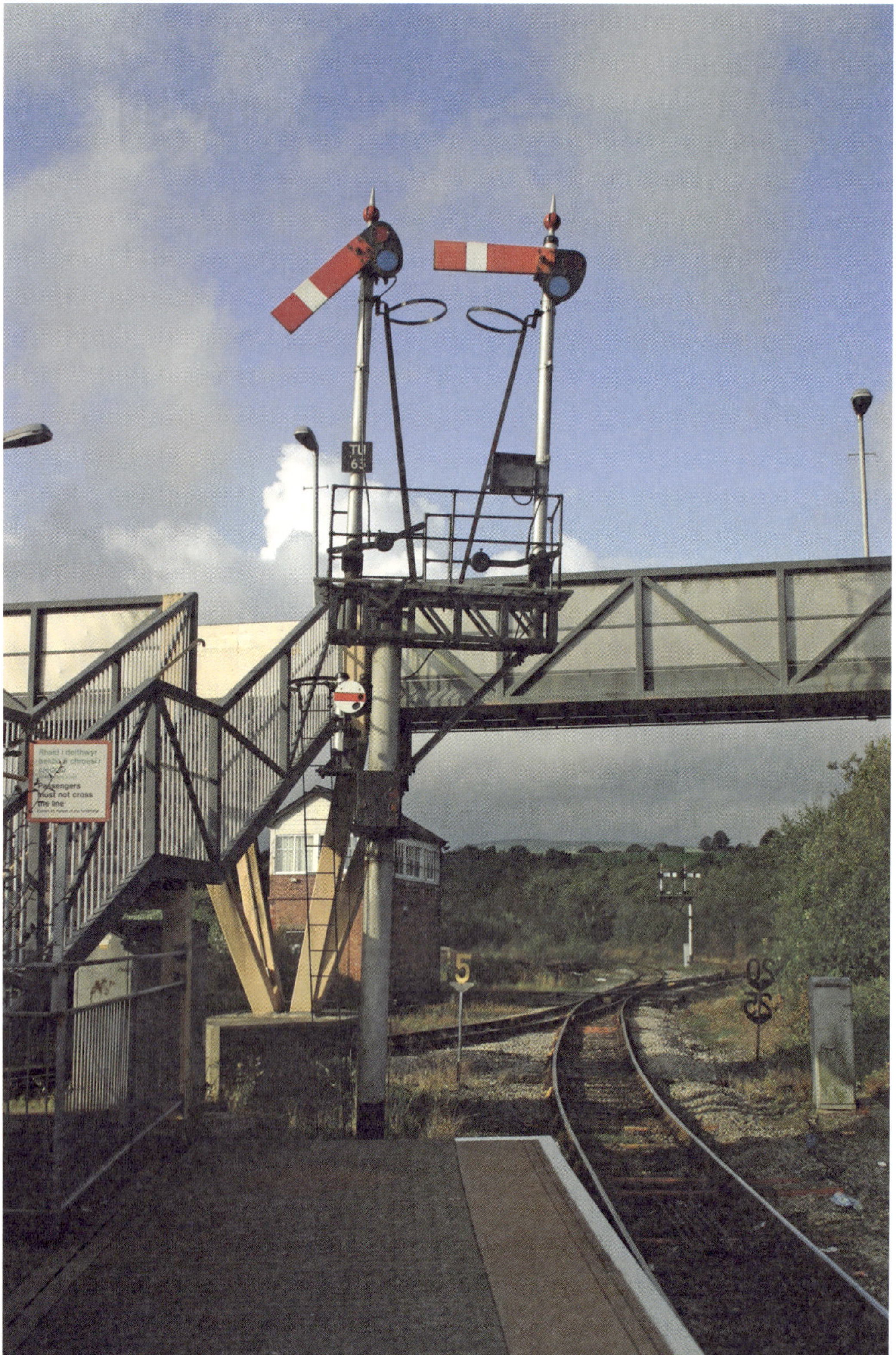
Rhaid i deithwyr
not cross
the line

A Contemporary Perspective on
GWR Signalling
Semaphore Swansong

Allen Jackson

THE CROWOOD PRESS

First published in 2015 by
The Crowood Press Ltd
Ramsbury, Marlborough
Wiltshire SN8 2HR

www.crowood.com

© Allen Jackson 2015

All rights reserved. No part of this publication may be reproduced or transmitted in any form or by any means, electronic or mechanical, including photocopy, recording, or any information storage and retrieval system, without permission in writing from the publishers.

British Library Cataloguing-in-Publication Data
A catalogue record for this book is available from the British Library.

ISBN 978 1 84797 949 0

Dedication
For Ninette.

Acknowledgements
The kindness and interest shown by railway signallers and the resident GWR expert at the Severn Valley Railway Museum, Kidderminster.

Frontispiece: Tondu station and the route
set for Maesteg, September 2006.

Typeset by Bookcraft Ltd, Stroud, Gloucestershire
Printed and bound in Malaysia by Times Offset (M) Sdn Bhd

Contents

	Preface	6
	Introduction	7
1	Lineside Signalling Equipment	9
2	Ways of Working	43
3	Signal Boxes and Infrastructure on Network Rail	50
	Worcester Area	51
	The Cotswold Line	61
	Worcester to Hereford	66
	Shrewsbury Area	71
	Shrewsbury to Hereford	78
	Hereford to Newport, South Wales	95
	North Warwickshire	103
	Worcester to Birmingham	112
	Chester to Wolverhampton	124
	Cornwall	136
	The Absorbed Lines	159
	Useful Resources	190
	Index	191

Preface

Although this book is largely a celebration of the past it could not have been written without twenty-first-century help.

After a long period of decline and neglect the railways are vital to many people's lives once more and it is right that the network be modernized and forward-looking.

The book has been written to appeal to the interested layperson rather than the signalling professional although grateful thanks are necessary to those people for their patient explanations of how it works.

Fig. 1 Class 66, 66 085 thunders through Craven Arms, Shropshire, heading north under clear signals on a Llanwern to Shotton steelworks working, August 2014.

Introduction

For over 150 years the safety, organization and efficient running of Britain's railways have relied on a system of semaphore signalling controlled from signal boxes, but by 2020, we are told, what remains of our rich heritage will no longer have a part in controlling the nation's network. This process of change has, however, been going on for around 100 years: in 1947, for example, there were about 10,000 signal boxes and in 2014 there were about 800 on Network Rail. By 2020 there will be fourteen.

Fig. 2   Looking at the jumble of signals from the Wolverhampton line towards Shrewsbury station with the largest mechanical signal box in the world at Severn Bridge Junction in the background, July 2014.

Luckily, in these islands, we have a preserved railway scene second to none and many of these railways have signalling systems that fully represent the semaphore and signal box scene that is so quickly disappearing from the national picture. The National Railway Museum at York has many signalling relics as well as the renowned Lancashire and Yorkshire Railway signalling school. In addition there is much signalling equipment in private hands and you can come across it almost anywhere.

The purpose of this volume is to present a record of the last of the operational mechanical signalling and infrastructure on our railway network as it applied to the former Great Western Railway including lines owned jointly with other companies.

Even at the outset the main lines in Britain had largely been modernised and it was a process begun in the 1960s. This has meant that large areas of the network have no mechanical signalling or signal boxes left and it has been so for some years now.

The GWR had its own way of doing things and some of that is retained to this day. Whilst most of the early railway companies sought to subcontract out the manufacture of signalling equipment, the GWR was ahead of its time in having its own signal works at Caversham Road in Reading. It was unusual in favouring the lower quadrant signal arm and persisting with that until the end of its existence on 31 December 1947. This means that the arm is normally at danger in the horizontal position (as on the title page photo at Worcester Shrub Hill), but when giving a Line Clear the arm drops down to below the horizontal. The Midland Railway and North Eastern Railways and others, which all disappeared in 1923 with the grouping of the railways into the 'Big Four', also favoured this style. The reason lower quadrant fell out of favour was to do with safety. Manually operated signals are usually worked by an iron rod called the down rod. The worry was that if this rod broke, a lower quadrant signal would naturally droop to show an OFF or clear indication and possibly cause an accident. It is always better if devices fail safely and it was felt a lower quadrant would not.

As originally the arms were made of wood the Great Western got round this problem by making the spectacle, or the thing that holds the lens, of heavy cast iron. This would counterbalance the weight of the arm should the down rod break and hold it at ON or danger.

In 2003, when I realised that the mechanical signalling way of life on our railways was coming to an end I started the photographic collection that has provided the material for the book. My survey eventually took in the whole of mainland Britain. This has brought us up to 2015 and material is still being enhanced and added to in the race to beat the clock.

CHAPTER 1

Lineside Signalling Equipment

Semaphore Signals

The Home Signal

The purpose of this signal could be described simply as stop or go. In the horizontal position the signal is said to be ON or stop. When the arm moves down from the horizontal by an angle of at least 60 degrees it is OFF or go.

The semaphore signal has evolved over time with operational experience and different materials used. Originally signal posts were made of wood, as were the arms. Posts since the 1940s are tubular steel and arms enamelled steel. The Western Region of British Railways continued with the steel style.

The oil lamp would originally be filled and trimmed every day, then later once a week and now they are electrically lit. The ladder was to allow access to the lamp and lens for cleaning. The post is finished off with a finial at the top, which apart from being decorative protects the timber post from the weather. Finials also appear on tubular post signals but more as decorative items.

The bottom few feet of the wooden post that is buried would be burned and charred to inhibit rot. Some wooden post signals survived into the 2000s so would have been at least sixty years old.

The example of the wooden post signal in Fig. 3 is at Carrog on the Llangollen Railway, in April 2008. The tapered wooden post is a reproduction and the signal arm has a distinctive 'swan neck' shape around the lens casting. This is classic GWR of the 1920s and 1930s and now exists only on the preserved railway scene.

Just about the last survivor of a wooden post GWR signal on Network Rail was at Shrewsbury, controlled by Crewe Junction signal box. It was still working in October 2003. It had lost its finial by this time and had replacement steel arms, as shown in Fig. 4.

Fig. 3 The down platform starter at Carrog, Llangollen Railway, protecting the route to Corwen, April 2008.

Fig. 4 One of the last wooden post GWR signals on Network Rail at Shrewsbury, October 2003.

Fig. 5 The 'go' condition displayed at Greenford East, London, April 2006.

Fig. 5 clearly illustrates a tubular post signal that is most definitely OFF or go. The lenses through which the lamp shines are red and blue as the original oil lamp would shine a yellow colour. When OFF the signal would then display a green light as required.

This is a cloistered enclave of semaphore signalling in west London which is surrounded by signalling modernity. Note the London Underground Limited (LUL) tube lines in the background. The rumblings of Crossrail are not far away.

Semaphore signals are usually operated by a series of wires and pulleys and bellcranks. A bellcrank is just a lever that lets a signal wire change direction and can amplify or diminish movement.

A similar principle is employed with points. All the equipment is connected to a lever in a signal box or sometimes to levers by the lineside known as a ground frame. In Fig. 6 the lever has a counterbalance weight that can be slid up and down the lever and then locked when the optimum balance position has been found. The signal technician will need this facility to set the signals up initially.

The lever operates the 'down rod', the black rod going vertically upwards which operates the signal arm. If the wire breaks the signal will return to ON or stop and is therefore failsafe. Fig. 7 shows the complete signal at Worcester Shrub Hill station.

The action of a train driver who passes a signal at danger is referred to as a SPAD (signal passed at danger) and this can have dire consequences. The Paddington rail crash of October 1999 was a SPAD

Fig. 6 The foot of a tubular steel signal post with the operating wires going round a pulley to operate the signal lever. There are two wires as there are two signals on this post. Worcester Shrub Hill station, July 2014.

Fig. 7 The complete signal at Worcester Shrub Hill station, July 2014.

and the cost was thirty-one people killed and over 400 injured. It was subsequently decided that the signal involved was badly sighted. There is a section on signal sighting later on in the Introduction.

The Distant Signal

A train that is moving fast and is heavy to the tune of several hundred tons possesses momentum, and this means any change in speed can take a while to take effect. The media will often compare it to a supertanker ship.

The distant signal is placed before the home signal to warn the train driver that the next signal might say stop and the distance between the signals gives the driver time to bring the train to a stand if needed.

A distant signal in the ON or horizontal position means proceed with caution and be prepared to stop at the next home signal. OFF means the next home signal is also OFF. The distance between home and distant signals is often a function of the maximum line speed: the higher the speed, the greater the distance between distant and home signals. In confined station areas, where speeds are low, the distance can be much reduced. The distance between a distant and home signal is often several hundred yards.

The yellow fishtailed distant signal is now quite rare and most certainly an endangered species. It has been largely replaced by colour light signals even in areas where semaphore home signals are prevalent. Colour lights are much easier to see in foggy and low light conditions and are considered safer.

In Fig. 8 the home signal is OFF but the distant is ON, meaning proceed past this signal but be prepared to stop at the next signal. This is a common means of slowing a train down when it is to take a slower line at the next junction signal. In this case the train is headed along the former Cambrian line, which is a slower-speed diverging route than straight on towards Hereford.

Fig. 8 A home and distant signal on one post. The home signal is saying proceed but the distant is saying proceed with caution and be prepared to stop at the next home signal. These signals are between Severn Bridge Junction and Sutton Bridge Junction Shrewsbury, July 2014.

Fig. 9 The same home and distant signal on one post as in Fig. 8. The home signal and distant signals together indicate proceed and expect the next home signal to be also OFF, Shrewsbury, July 2014.

In Fig. 9 the train is obviously going down the Hereford line as both 'boards' are off. Note the modernized ladders and hoops on this Shrewsbury signal.

Some parts of the former GWR, Western Region British Railways, were hived off to other regions. Some of the area around Shrewsbury became London Midland Region from the 1960s and so other influences have been creeping in. Upper quadrant signals similar to ex-LMS designs are to be seen.

The distant signal in Fig. 10 is an upper quadrant at Sutton Bridge Junction Shrewsbury but the two signals behind it on the opposite track are still lower quadrant. This distant signal is fixed at caution, meaning the next home signal nearer Shrewsbury station may be ON so proceed with caution.

These signals, which are permanently at caution, are referred to as 'fixed distants'. This is why there is no lens in the OFF position. The signal is never OFF so it doesn't need one.

As mentioned above, the distant would be ON to slow a train for the lower speed at a junction. The bracket signal on the right of the picture is the junction in question, with the right-hand arm for the Cambrian and the left for Hereford branch.

Before Word War I GWR distant signal arms were red with the fishtail shape.

The Calling On Signal Arm

In Fig. 10 there is a smaller arm with red and white stripes below the home and distant arms. The purpose of this is to enable a train to enter a track where a train may already be standing, for example where two fairly short trains will occupy the same platform at a station. This is fairly commonplace as trains in recent years have got shorter but more frequent.

The mode of operation is to leave the home signal ON or at danger and bring the train to a stand. The signaller then sets the calling on arm to clear or OFF. This is to signify to the driver to proceed with the utmost caution.

Calling on arms are never used outside station areas where speeds are usually much higher and the required manoeuvre is not needed. Fig. 11 is a very modern incarnation of lower quadrant home signal and calling on arm.

There is a refinement to the calling on arm, using a device that can convey additional information, as shown in Fig. 12. The indicator is used to display either a C or a W character. A C tells the train driver to expect the platform to be occupied by another train further down towards the end. The W is to warn the train driver that although the platform may be clear, the track after the home signal that the platform is controlled by is blocked. This is an additional safety precaution lest the driver should overrun or pass the home signal at danger. The colloquial term for this indicator is a 'stencil box'.

Ground Disc Signals

These signals are usually used to signal a manoeuvre across a crossover, where a train moves from one running line to the other, or to enter a siding or loop line. Loop lines are used to store trains temporarily while they are overtaken by a faster train or to quarantine a train that has broken down. Access to loops can also be by conventional running signals.

The term ground disc is universally used despite the fact that some signals are now raised from the ground to be at or near the same level as normal running signals. It does make sense that the track would be easier to follow if the signals are at a

Fig. 10   Upper quadrant home and distant signals, with calling on arm below them on the same post at Sutton Bridge Junction Shrewsbury, July 2014.

Fig. 11   Home and calling on arms controlling the entry to Shrewsbury station platform 7 from the Crewe line. Crewe Junction signal box, Shrewsbury, July 2014.

Fig. 12   Bracket signal controlling entry to Shrewsbury station from the Chester line, July 2014.

Fig. 13 Ground disc controlling entry to goods loop at Craven Arms Crossing, south Shropshire, August 2014.

Fig. 14 Double-decker ground disc signals, upper quadrant, Sutton Bridge Junction Shrewsbury, July 2014.

and being on the left side of the locomotive, would be able to see the aspect. The GWR had such a device as a backing signal, and these can still be found in preservation at Bridgnorth and Bewdley on the Severn Valley Railway. They were often found together with a route indicator or cash register to signify which of several routes the train was reversing down.

The signal is wire operated and you can see the wire disappearing up to the top right-hand corner of the picture. Part-way down the wire is a steel bar, and the purpose of this is to slot into another bar at right angles which is attached to the point or turnout in question. These are detection slide bars.

This bar at right angles has slots cut into it that coincide with a slot cut into the ground disc bar. This locks the ground disc to display only the correct indication relative to the point's position. This feature of interlocking is a universal safety feature in railway signalling and one we shall return to later.

The signal has a standard electric lamp fitting of plastic with LEDs for illumination.

Ground discs can be stacked up, one above the other, as in Fig. 14; in this case the lower disc refers to the track nearest the driver and the upper disc to the one further away. This arrangement harks back to earlier days when subsidiary signals in shunting yards or station areas would be arranged one above the other. I seem to recall the maximum on one post was six signals.

A ground disc can even have a different-coloured disc, as in Figs 15 and 16. This is where it is required that a locomotive or train passes the disc when it is ON where there is repetitive shunting going on to avoid the signaller having to change the aspect of the disc signal every time the train approaches the disc. Railways in the past have referred to such relaxations as 'permissive' working. A calling on arm may be thought of this way. These permissive signals were much more common in steam days when most trains would be shunted at some point. More recently, trains are described as a 'block' or in sets and so shunting is much reduced and the need

uniform height. On the other hand, there is also a view that placing these signals up with the running signals might confuse drivers, particularly at night. There is no set policy, however, and the final arbiter is always the visibility to a driver of a signal.

In Fig. 13 there is a ground signal almost right on the crossing at Craven Arms, which controls the reverse entry to the goods loop. The normal way of entry is by ordinary running signals on posts – left to right in the picture. This signal enables a train to reverse into the loop. It is on the right-hand side of the track, as the driver looks back while reversing,

Fig. 15   Black ground disc with a yellow stripe at Worcester Shrub Hill station, July 2014.

Fig. 16   Black ground disc with a yellow stripe at Moreton-in-Marsh station, Gloucestershire, September 2009.

for such signals is consequently reduced. They are now quite rare.

When a ground disc is not a ground disc in terms of its position it can be referred to colloquially as a disc or dolly or even a ground dolly. A signal on a post is sometimes referred to as a doll and perhaps a diminutive of doll is dolly. Anyway, elevated ground discs, as in Fig. 17, are becoming increasingly common compared with their lower altitude cousins.

Fig. 18 shows a good example of an elevated ground disc at Par in Cornwall; the lamp appears to be a converted oil lamp.

Another ground signal is shown in Fig. 19 and this is included because it illustrates a principle of signalling that has a wider use than just ground discs.

The pivot lug that holds the ground disc can clearly be seen, especially the vacant one halfway up the post. At the pivot that is in use there is a white, curvy plate that clearly rotates when the signal is operated. The purpose of this plate is to obscure the small rearward-facing light that shines out of the black plastic box with the cable hanging from it. This indicates to the signaller, whose signal box is off to the right of the picture, that the ground disc has operated.

Fig. 17   Elevated ground discs coming off the Chester line, Crewe Junction signal box, July 2014.

15

LINESIDE SIGNALLING EQUIPMENT

Fig. 18 Elevated ground disc on a bracket signal at Par station, Cornwall, October 2004.

Fig. 19 Rear view of a ground signal at Shrewsbury station. This signal is controlled by Severn Bridge Junction signal box, July 2014.

Signaller feedback is important and the signaller must be told what the actual status of the equipment is, irrespective of what controls have been operated in the signal box. This curvy plate is known as a 'backlight blinder' or 'backlight cover' and is only used on signals that can be seen by the signaller from the rear. Signals that face the signaller or are out of sight altogether do not usually have this feature. With signals that are out of sight, the signaller is advised of the signal's position by other means, which are covered later in the book.

Brackets and Gantries

Bracket Signals

A bracket signal can be described as more than one signal mounted on one central post but with separate posts for each signal. A gantry is a construction that spans at least two tracks and has at least two posts in the ground to support a bridge-like structure. As gantries tend to be bespoke to their location they are more expensive to maintain and the policy in recent years has been to replace gantries wherever possible with multiples of bracket signals.

The bracket signal is used to signal diverging routes and the usual maximum now is a total of three routes. The height of the signals relative to one another tells the train driver what the relative speeds of the diverging routes are, as the curvature of a diverging route very often requires a lower speed than straight on. In addition the actual speeds of the various routes are spelled out on lineside discs or the earlier stencil figures, similar to road speed restriction signs.

The size of the signal arm also tells the train driver the type of route for that particular branch. For example, a 4ft arm is a passenger-carrying line and a 3ft arm is for freight or goods or locomotives on their own. In GWR days a loop or goods line would have a painted white ring on the smaller arm to indicate a lesser function. These can still be seen at Bridgnorth on the Severn Valley Railway.

Fig. 20 shows a bracket signal at Woofferton Junction between Shrewsbury and Hereford, where there is a goods loop. The 4ft right-hand signal is the up passenger-carrying line towards Shrewsbury. The smaller 3ft arm is for entry to the goods loop on the left at a lower speed. You can also see the speed restriction sign for 15mph, referring to the goods loop entry. Note the most unusual finials on both posts; they look like Westinghouse Brake and Signal Company products.

Fig. 21 shows the three-way bracket signal controlled by Crewe Junction signal box at Shrewsbury. The signal is located coming off the Crewe line and indicates whether the train is to go into platform 4 or 7, or the passing loop that avoids the platforms

Fig. 20 Bracket signal at Woofferton Junction on the Hereford–Shrewsbury line, August 2014.

altogether. Reading from left to right it would be loop, platform 7, platform 4. The wires coming away from the girder platform are like guy ropes on a tent, there simply to steady the structure.

The backlight blinders behind the arms show up well here and are needed, as Crewe Junction box is some way behind the signal post to the left of the picture.

Back to Worcester Shrub Hill station now and another three-doll bracket signal in Fig. 22. The doll on the left is for the line to Hereford via Worcester Foregate station. This is approached on a curve, which explains the lower height of the post.

The centre 3ft arm is even lower and that is because it leads straight to the locomotive sidings, which are only a little way from the station and so caution is necessary.

The post or doll on the far right is the Birmingham line out of the station and is the fastest line of the three. All the distant signals are fixed as this is in a station area and these distants do not even have spectacles or lenses, just a yellow lamp that shines ahead.

Fig. 23 is more of a historical piece than one containing any novelty except that the signal arms are not only wood but are centre balanced but still lower quadrant. This means that the arms are not pivoted at the ends but in the centre of the arm. This gives rise to a curious position for the blue lens. You can clearly see that the wooden arms are clinging on to their existence thanks to some steel strapping supports. Centre-balanced arms are used where space is at a premium and quite often on platforms where a full-length arm might strike a passenger when in the OFF position. Clearly visible are the bellcranks that transmit the movement of the signal wire from the signal box up through a tube to rods via the bellcranks and then to the signal arm. On the left-hand signal, which is easier to follow, the rod connected to the arm must go up to move the arm off. If you follow it through you should be able

Fig. 21 Triple-armed bracket signal controlling the entry to Shrewsbury station off the Crewe line, July 2014.

17

LINESIDE SIGNALLING EQUIPMENT

to see that the rod behind the SBJ plate must also go up to move the arm to the OFF position.

The signals control the exit from platform 7 at Shrewsbury station. The left-hand arm is for Wellington and Wolverhampton and the right for the crossovers to Sutton Bridge Junction and the Hereford and Cambrian lines.

Bracket signals don't always have multiple signal arms on them. In the example shown at Newport, Park Junction in Fig. 24, the signal on the right is of the bracket form because of sighting by the train driver. This is becoming a common theme – many variations in signal placing and ancillary equipment are to do with driver sighting. Both bracket signals are conventionally situated to the left of the line they serve.

Park Junction signal box has 100 signal levers.

A further example of a driver sighting bracket signal is the example outside Worcester Foregate Street station in Fig. 25. This seemingly rather odd configuration for double track is explained by the fact that these are two single lines. The one on the left goes to Droitwich Spa and the one on the right to Worcester Shrub Hill station. The sighting bracket to Shrub Hill also has a fixed distant on the same

Fig. 22 Triple bracket signal at Worcester Shrub Hill station, November 2008.

Fig. 23 Bracket signal with centre-balanced arms, Shrewsbury station, September 2005.

18

Fig. 24 A pair of bracket signals outside Newport Park Junction signal box, South Wales, August 2006.

post. The bracket signal would normally be on the left of the track it serves but once again, for sighting reasons and ease of maintenance, the post has been placed on the right.

As these are single lines where traffic can run in either direction on either line, the line is also signalled in both directions.

Gantry Signals

Gantries have become something of a rarity, and only the one controlled by Crewe Junction signal box at Shrewsbury, shown in Fig. 26, is offered for study. It controls the movement from platforms 3 and 4 and the through line from Wolverhampton to the Chester and Crewe lines. Originally there

Fig. 25 A signal sighting bracket outside Worcester Foregate station, March 2004.

Fig. 26   Gantry facing the Crewe and Chester lines, Shrewsbury station, October 2003.

was a semaphore doll for each possible route that could be taken and that added up to ten as recently as the 1950s. However, with the colour light 'theatre' route indicators this has been reduced to just three signals in all. Even the remaining semaphore signal has lost its finial, which is distinctly un-Shrewsbury-like.

The illuminated theatre-type route indicator has been around since at least the 1950s and it uses a matrix of bulbs that are selected to indicate a route in the form of a letter, for example, M for main. These are still around but in a more modern format have ultra-bright light-emitting diodes (LEDs) that form the letter display, and some have fibre-optics. LEDs have a longer service life than filament bulbs and consume less power per unit, and the same is true for fibre-optics.

Semaphore gantries are, however, making a minor comeback, with a fine example at Kidderminster station on the Severn Valley Railway.

Route Indicator

When you have more than two diverging routes a gantry or multiple bracket is needed to display all the options, each with their own arm. This is more costly to construct and perhaps confusing to a train driver. The other issue can be one of space at the trackside.

A solution to this is the route indicator that is known colloquially in the signalling industry as a 'cash register'. This is because the action of pulling a lever in the signal box raises a caption in the white-backed box below the signal arm. In the example in Figs 27 and 28 at Worcester Shrub Hill it could have offered three options – B'HAM, H'FRD or LOCO. These are abbreviations for Birmingham, Hereford or the locomotive depot. This is a historic situation in that LOCO is no longer required, and if you look carefully at the number of levers below the black caption box you will see there are now only two, for the other two destinations. The caption box was originally lit from behind by an oil lamp.

This signal is the starter at the end of platform 2, whereas paradoxically at the end of platform 1 is the full bracket array for the three destinations. Perhaps there wasn't room for all that again on the adjacent platform. These arrays form the front cover page for this book.

These signals in this form are now very rare and the only surviving example on Network Rail is at Worcester Shrub Hill.

There had been another at Yeovil Pen Mill in Somerset but this has been replaced by a Southern

Fig. 27 Sole surviving Network Rail 'cash register' signal, Worcester Shrub Hill, November 2008.

Fig. 28 Rear view of the route indicator at Worcester Shrub Hill, July 2014.

Region bracket signal, as this place also lost its loco depot and so only two destinations were needed. Yeovil Pen Mill is on the route from Castle Cary to Weymouth and this had been transferred to the Southern Region in the 1960s.

These signals tended to be in lower-speed areas such as stations or shunting yards. The first recorded occurrence of their use was at Paddington station in 1909, where a six-route cash register was installed to control empty coaching stock movements into the platforms, numbered 1 to 6.

Motorized Signals

So far we have only considered signalling operation in terms of wires pulled from a lever in a signal box and then a counterbalance weight returning the signal to danger when the lever is returned. Some signals, because of distance from the signal box or other operational reasons, may have to be remotely worked by electric motor. In the earlier days, before mains electricity was commonplace, motor-worked signals and indeed points could be

Fig. 29   Looking towards Hereford from Craven Arms station platform. The signal number 1 is on the right and in the distance with its back to the camera, August 2014.

energized by a small generator usually referred to as a 'hurdy gurdy' as it had to be manually cranked. Nowadays motorized devices are mains driven and signal boxes are equipped with uninterruptible power supply (UPS), which is basically batteries that supply mains standby power through a device called an inverter. Inverters are commonly available to run mains equipment in cars and caravans.

The first example (Fig. 29) of a motorized signal is signal number 1 at Craven Arms Crossing signal box, which, although it is a home signal, is 1,211yd (1,107m) from the signal box. The signal is pulled with a conventional lever, which operates an

Fig. 30   Gobowen down platform starter for Chester. Note the motor on the post above the signal arm. Gobowen North signal box is across the crossing, August 2004.

Fig. 31 Side view of Gobowen North signal number 4 (GN4), November 2004.

Fig. 32 Motor-worked home signal, Worcester Tunnel Junction signal box, April 2005.

electrical switch that drives the motor to pull the signal off for an approaching train. When the train has passed, a sensor at the trackside returns the signal to the danger position automatically. The signaller still has to return the signal lever back in the frame manually.

Next we go north to Gobowen near the Welsh border between Shrewsbury and Chester. In this example this signal is motor driven by a motor up the post, even though Gobowen North signal box is across the road.

This was because the proximity of the crossing was thought to be a hazard to normal signal wires and there was a fear of vandalism at this location.

Worcester Tunnel Junction signal box controls the home signal on the up main line towards Shrub Hill station, shown in Fig. 32. This time the motor is at the bottom of the post. This is unusual in that the signal box is just behind the photographer so it's not a distance thing. This is more likely to be related to automatic operation to safeguard the entry to the station.

Banjo Signals

In an environment where regular-sized arms are not appropriate and the background clutter would make a conventional signal arm difficult to spot by a train driver, there is a large 32in (81cm) disc signal available, as in Fig. 33. This is another area where Worcester Shrub Hill can claim to have the only working example left on Network Rail. This signal controls the up platform movements. Note the half-size calling on arm below is not striped but simply inscribed CO instead. This lettering of signal arms harks back to earlier days. Just two

Fig. 33 Banjo disc and calling on arm at Worcester Shrub Hill station, July 2014.

Fig. 34 Bellcrank and wire detail from the banjo disc and calling on arm Worcester Shrub Hill station, November 2008.

Fig. 35 Evesham's E33 signal on the wrong side of the tracks, with lower-mounted arm and smaller-size 3ft arm, March 2004.

wires operate the 32in banjo disc and the calling on arm.

Originally the track layout was more complicated, as can be seen from the redundant bellcranks on the wall at Worcester Shrub Hill station.

The Sighting of Signals

A good deal of time and energy is spent making sure that train drivers can see signals clearly and in good time to take action. We've seen some of it already.

Very often a signal position is changed or additional equipment is employed to help sighting after train crews have commented on their view, or lack of one, of the signals.

Where driving is on the left, traffic lights or road signals are commonly on the left, and so it is with railways unless there is a reason to change it. In Fig. 35 we have a home signal – in fact the plate on the post tells us it is Evesham's signal number 33 – and the signal is halfway down the post, is smaller and has a centre-balanced arm as opposed to side-mounted. Furthermore, the signal refers to the left-hand side tracks and yet is positioned by the right-hand side track.

All these differences are to aid sighting of the signal by a train driver.

In Fig. 36 we can see the reason for all the changes. The view is from the train driver's approximate position and the position of the road overbridge explains all. If the signal was sighted on the left and at a typical post height the driver would never see it. The red and white chequerboard on the bridge arch is to warn of limited clearance.

Sometimes it is not necessary to move the signal to the other side of the track or the arm down the post but just highlight the view, as the background may be such that the signal view is lost in clutter and therefore difficult to see. Sighting boards are sometimes used to highlight the background to a signal's position. Two such signals fitted with sighting boards on the approach to Shrewsbury station from Chester are shown in Fig. 37. The signals control access to the up main goods loop (left-hand signal) and platform 7 (right-hand signal).

It used to be commonplace to whitewash a road overbridge that was directly behind a signal to improve sighting. That is not so common now.

In the next example a special installation is necessary due to the nature of the station shelter and the sheer rock face behind the platform. Fig. 38 features the up starter at Liskeard station in Cornwall; 'up' here refers to towards London, whereas 'down' is towards Penzance. 'Starter' means it is the entry point to the next block section (*see* Chapter 2). The signaller cannot lower this signal until permission has been granted from the next signal box along the line.

This lower quadrant signal is shown OFF. It is made of wood and so is a rarity.

Fig. 36   The reason for Evesham's E33 signal being engineered so distinctively can be seen – and so can the signal, March 2004.

Fig. 37   A pair of home signals with sighting boards coming off the Chester line into Shrewsbury station, July 2014.

These signals at Craven Arms in Fig. 39 have had exceptionally long posts fitted to the bracket so that the train driver can see the signals above the bridge that the photographer is standing on. The signals control the entry to the down section at Craven Arms and the main line is pulled off for a class 175 Coradia DMU, which is heading for the Hereford direction. The smaller 3ft arm on the left is to control entry to the down goods loop.

Fig. 38 A centre-balanced starter signal at Liskeard, Cornwall, March 2004.

Fig. 39 A tall bracket signal approaching Craven Arms in the direction of Hereford, August 2014.

Fig. 40 A sighting board and calling on arm from the rear at Worcester Shrub Hill station, July 2014.

Another home signal plus sighting board is shown in Fig. 40, this time from the rear together with a calling on arm at Worcester Shrub Hill station, the up main signal from the Birmingham route.

Banner Repeater

Another device to aid the sighting of running signals is a different type of signal. The banner repeater is used to repeat the aspect of a signal that is too difficult to see until it's too late. It gives an advance warning of what is to come and is often found on lines of severe curvature, where making the posts taller or shorter and so forth would not solve the problem.

Fig. 41 is a banner repeater signal on platform 4 at Shrewsbury station and the signal it refers to or duplicates is CJ97, which is the signal on the far right of the gantry at the end of the platform. Fig. 42 is simply the rear of CJ97. The signal is electrically operated and lit.

Fig. 43 attempts to illustrate the difficulty of sighting CJ97 and why the banner repeater is there. The view is across to platform 4 where the banner repeater is, and the signal is just visible above the red Royal Mail parcel trolleys. You can see the gantry to which it refers, and CJ97 is on the far right of the gantry. Crewe Junction signal box is in the background. By this later date the banner repeater signal has been replaced by an LED version.

A standalone banner repeater is to be found at the south end of Gobowen station, and this is the repeater for GN4, the motorized signal shown in Figs 30 and 31. Fig. 44 shows the rear view but you can clearly see the aspect is ON or at danger. The track curving away to the right in the distance is the Oswestry branch.

Fig. 41 Banner repeater on platform 4 at Shrewsbury station, September 2005.

Fig. 42 (right centre) Rear of the banner repeater on platform 4 at Shrewsbury station, September 2005.

Fig. 43 (below) Looking across at platform 4 to the banner repeater and signal gantry, Shrewsbury station, July 2014.

LINESIDE SIGNALLING EQUIPMENT

Fig. 44   Banner repeater at the south end of Gobowen station, November 2004.

Fig. 45   Fibre-optic banner repeater controlled by Worcester Tunnel Junction signal box, April 2005.

Fig. 46   Fibre-optic banner repeater controlled by Worcester Tunnel Junction signal box with the home signal it duplicates in the background, April 2005.

The last banner repeater (Figs 45 and 46) is a modern fibre-optic version and this is located on the line from Droitwich to Worcester Foregate station near Rainbow Hill junction. A fibre-optic device permits light from a single source to be sent down many fibres to aggregate in a display.

This signal is controlled by Worcester Tunnel Junction signal box. The home signal that it is duplicating is beyond and behind the signal housing.

Signalling Feedback

Signal Position

We have seen so far how a signaller can be given feedback that the signal has answered the lever by the use of a backlight blinder if the rear of the signal is facing the signaller and is visible from the signal box.

Other signals, which are not visible from the signal box, still have to be reported to the signaller as to their status, OFF or ON.

A device attached to the signal pivot transmits the position of the signal. Fig. 47 shows this. Behind the signal post is a silver-painted (or sometimes

Fig. 47   Rear of the home signal at Leominster showing the position transmitter, August 2014.

black) rectangular box that contains the transmitter that will send back the signal position. Below the silver-painted box is a black slider that is coupled to the signal arm pivot. As the arm pivot rotates the slider moves up and down, altering the position fed back to the signal box. This signal is at Leominster

Fig. 48   Instrument shelf at Craven Arms showing home signals all ON, August 2014.

on the Shrewsbury–Hereford line and is only yards from the signal box, but the bridge that the photographer is standing on obscures the view of what the arm is doing.

At the signal box the transmitted signal is shown as either ON or OFF. WRONG would mean there has been a power failure to the instrument. Fig. 48 depicts instruments in Craven Arms signal box. Signals 1 (*see* Fig. 29), 2 and 4 are all in the ON position. The numbers come from the signal diagram present in every signal box.

An ex-GWR signaller described the yellow round device in Figs 49 and 50 as 'that Midland contraption', but it does the same job as the rectangular silver-painted box. This is Severn Bridge Junction signal leading towards the Hereford and Cambrian lines at Shrewsbury.

Lamp Status

Lamps are fitted with forward-facing and backward-facing lights so that the lamp status can be checked where visible. Where the lamp is not

Fig. 49 Rear of signals between Severn Bridge Junction and Sutton Bridge Junction. Note the yellow position transmitters, July 2014.

Fig. 50 Front view of signals between Severn Bridge Junction and Sutton Bridge Junction. Note the yellow position transmitters, July 2014.

visible to the signaller in either respect another device is required.

The original oil lamps were fitted with a bimetallic strip. When two dissimilar metals are clamped together, their differing rates of expansion due to heat cause the strip to bow and bend. This principle is used in thermostats around the home but here the strip is placed above the oil lamp burner and so long as the lamp is lit no indication is sent. As soon as the lamp goes out the strip makes an electrical contact, which shows in the signal box as 'lamp out', and it can also ring a bell. At night a lamp out is the same as having no signal at all.

As lamps now tend to be electric, a circuit that senses current flow is used to power the same indicators. If there is no current flow the lamp has failed or, more improbably, the circuit has failed.

Again, in addition to the indicator a bell can ring to indicate a lamp out. Some of these indicators are wired in parallel to monitor more than one signal. This is simply to save on the amount of equipment needed and space on the shelf in the signal box.

On receipt of an alarm the signaller or signal technician has to determine which is actually faulty. Fig. 51 depicts a venerable GWR lamp out indicator made of mahogany with some brass fittings. This instrument would be at home in a Victorian drawing room as it is just about from that era.

This venerability translates into cash, as these items, and indeed most of what appears in a signal box, are highly prized collector's items. Note the knob at the front to switch the bell off. This is at Craven Arms signal box and signal 9, to which the ivorine plate on the front of the indicator refers. It is the branch home, which is the semaphore home signal that controls the exit from the Central Wales line from Pantyffynon and Swansea. The indicator is displaying the LAMP IN caption. Next to it on the left is a more modern incarnation of a lamp out indicator from the 1940s or 1950s.

A more prosaic and consequently less valuable collector's piece from Craven Arms signal box is depicted in Fig. 52. It looks as though the device has been adapted from a distant signal status indicator

Fig. 51 Lamp out indicator at Craven Arms signal box, August 2014.

but actually shows the lamp status of the up colour light distant signal towards Shrewsbury. The signal is number 100 according to the ivorine disc, so this lamp out indicator is also, in effect, a signal status indicator.

The instrument can display the pointer to show light on (that is, signal yellow light showing), light off (signal green light showing) or not working.

The signal is 2,984yd (2,729m) from the signal box with its back to the signaller and over the brow of a hill. Fig. 29 gives you an idea as to how far away this signal is from the box.

The indicator on the left of the status/lamp out machine displays the state of the UPS. If the mains has failed the status/lamp out device will display normally but the signaller needs to know if the UPS

Fig. 52 Distant signal colour light status indicator, Craven Arms, August 2014.

has kicked in because it too will fail when the batteries flatten.

Note signals 100, 1 and 2 are OFF, which means a train is signalled to run through the section at normal line speed, which can be up to 90mph here, depending on the type of train. If signal 100 was ON, the train driver would be checked and slowed.

Other Signalling Variations

Here are some oddities that exist on the former GWR network that have been observed and photographed.

Hitherto on running lines the default condition has always been: if there isn't a train imminent then the signals are at danger. At Worcester Shrub Hill through freight loop the opposite is the case (Figs 53 and 54). There are two semaphore home signals that are nearly always OFF. They are controlled by a separate ground frame from Worcester Shrub Hill signal box. Occasionally a freight train will pull into the loop line to run round so that it can set off in the opposite direction to which it arrived. When that happens and a freight train enters the loop, the signals will be replaced to danger to protect the train.

Fig. 55 is more of a sign than a signal placed by one of the sidings, and is known as a 'limit of shunt indicator'. In other words it means no locomotive can pass the STOP sign at any time.

Still at Worcester Shrub Hill station, there is another minor oddity at the Oxford end of platform 2. The bay siding beside platform 2 is usually used to stable a DMU set. It has the starter signal number SH11 to let it out onto the up main line as shown in Fig. 56. Almost by the side of it is signal SH7, so to avoid confusion, SH11 has what appears to be a sighting board attached to it to mask the aspect of SH7 to a driver who should be looking at SH11 to move off onto the main line.

Now we head south and west to South Wales and Newport Park Junction signal box area, shown in Fig. 57. To prevent unauthorized access to the signal arm and lamp the ladder has been locked with a timber board fitted to the signal ladder.

This is a view from the part of the Ebbw Vale line that is double track looking south towards Park Junction and the box. The line to Machen, which ends up at a quarry, is on the right. The disc at the bottom of the post signals the Machen branch and the home signal for the down line to Ebbw Vale

LINESIDE SIGNALLING EQUIPMENT

Fig. 53   Freight or goods loop line signal OFF with STOP indicator behind it on siding, Worcester Shrub Hill station, November 2008.

Fig. 54   Freight or goods loop line signal OFF, in the distance, Worcester Shrub Hill station, November 2008.

Fig. 55 STOP indicator on freight siding, Worcester Shrub Hill station, November 2008.

Fig. 56 DMU stabling point bay starter signal masking the display from the adjacent platform, Worcester Shrub Hill station, July 2014.

itself. Subsequent to the survey the Ebbw Vale line has been reinstated for passengers.

Not so much a variation as a historical rarity, the GWR ground signal in Fig. 58 that controls part of the exit from the former Motorail bays at Worcester Shrub Hill Station has a smaller disc and an arched bifurcated foot as opposed to the flat webbed slab of the BR or Network Rail version. It looks like it has a genuine oil lamp, but it is a conversion.

Fig. 59 depicts signal DS73 at Droitwich Spa, which is protecting the junction with the line to Bromsgrove and Birmingham and in the direction of Worcester.

It appears that a modernization using the galvanized hoops and renewed platform was started and then abandoned. Perhaps the signal is too tall for the modern fittings. The tendency in recent years has been to lower signals wherever possible on health and safety grounds, assuming all else being equal with regard to sighting.

At Bromfield near Ludlow in south Shropshire, the home signal in Fig. 60 demonstrates that the basic build of a signal can be changed around to suit the conditions on-site. The ladder normally faces to the rear of a signal, parallel with the track line, while here it is at 90 degrees to the track line.

Fig. 57   Goods or loop line signal with anti-climb apparatus fitted, Newport Park Junction, August 2006.

Fig. 58   GWR ground disc signal at Worcester Shrub Hill station, October 2003.

Fig. 60   Side-mounted ladder on home signal at Bromfield near Ludlow, July 2014.

Fig. 59   Signal DS73 at Droitwich Spa almost modernized, July 2014.

The up goods loop at Woofferton Junction between Shrewsbury and Leominster is protected by a home and loop goods signal, as depicted in Fig. 61. However, the way in which the signal position status is passed to the signal box is unusual. There is a cranked arm connecting the signal arm directly to the position transmitter.

Fig. 62 shows Sutton Bridge Junction, Shrewsbury, and we have been here before. The bracket signal on the right seems out of balance somehow and that is because there used to be three posts on the bracket. Up until September 1963 there was a branch line from Shrewsbury to Kidderminster and this point on the junction is

35

Fig. 61 Unusual position transmitter cranks on signals at Woofferton Junction, south Shropshire, July 2014.

where it left the main line. Part of it has been re-opened and is now the Severn Valley Railway. When a line is closed, the signal arm only is removed in the first instance, rather than the signal post.

Topical Tracks

So far this work has been just about signals but it is becoming clearer that signals and track are intertwined and interdependent. Although they are termed signal boxes, many track functions are managed and interlocked with the signalling system. Certain track conditions are needed before signals can operate. All this is to ensure a safer railway and has stood the test of time for about 140 years. It has been integrated with more modern technology to maintain an outstanding record for the travelling public.

Points – Facing and Trailing

As far as signalling is concerned, points on running lines – as opposed to sidings or loops which are not on running lines – are divided up into two main categories: facing points, whose blades face the

Fig. 62 Bracket signal, on the right, that used to control Severn Valley route. Sutton Bridge Junction Shrewsbury, July 2014.

LINESIDE SIGNALLING EQUIPMENT

Fig. 63   Trailing and facing points forming crossovers at Woofferton Junction near Ludlow, southern Shropshire, August 2014.

oncoming train, and trailing points, whose blades are trailed by the oncoming train. In Fig. 63 we have examples of both at Woofferton Junction near Ludlow.

As you can see from the running signals, the left-hand line starts at the bottom of the picture and goes northwards towards Shrewsbury towards the top of the picture.

The first pair of points, forming a crossover between the two tracks, is a trailing points pair. The next pair up, going northwards up the picture, are facing points. Their blades, or the things that move to change over, are facing the oncoming train in both directions.

This is important because it was found, very early on in the history of the railways, that the force of a train hitting facing points can, under certain circumstances, force the point blades to open and cause a derailment. The GWR avoided facing points on running lines wherever possible because of such fears.

Where facing points are unavoidable on running lines they are fitted with a locking mechanism that locks the point blades in whichever position they are selected. Facing point locks occupy another lever in a signal box for every set of facing points there are, and signals are interlocked not only with points but with facing point locks where they are found.

Fig. 64 depicts the facing point lock mechanism of part of the facing crossover at Woofferton Junction, shown in the previous figure. The rectangular rod coming in from the left of the picture and turning through 90 degrees with a bellcrank

Fig. 64   Facing point arrangements at Woofferton Junction near Ludlow, southern Shropshire, August 2014.

37

Fig. 65 Facing point locking detail at Shrewsbury station, July 2014.

to the point blades is what transmits movement to the point from the lever in the signal box. The same movement is transmitted across to the facing point on the other track, via more bellcranks, as these points are co-acting. In other words they cannot operate by themselves individually and there is no circumstance where they ever would.

Before any movement of any of the facing points can take place, though, the rectangular rod coming in from the top of the picture must move towards you, the reader. This is transmitted via the bellcrank bolted to the sleeper to the rectangular rod running at right angles to the sleepers. This has the action of withdrawing a locking bar that stops the point blades from moving. The signaller can now change the points but must replace the locking bar afterwards to relock the points in their new position.

So the movement is:

1. Undo facing point lock.
2. Move point over to new position.
3. Replace facing point lock.

For this crossover there will be one lever for the crossover and one for the facing point locks.

The additional rectangular rodding coming towards you in the picture are detection slides that ensure that the point is in position and locked before any ground disc signal can be pulled off. The main running signals and points and facing point locks are interlocked at the signal box. Trailing points are interlocked with signals but clearly have no need of facing point locks.

Fig. 65 shows how a facing point lock can work a bit better. The tie bar holding the two point blades apart has two slots cut into it. You can just see one of them to the right of the facing point lock housing, which is the shiny rectangle bolted to a sleeper in the middle of the rails. The facing point lock bolt engages with one of the slots and stops the tie bar, and hence the point blades, from moving. From this it is easy to see that the lock must be pulled out before the point can be changed over.

When single lines are considered and trains normally run on the same track in both directions, any point on a running line must be a facing point in one direction.

Trap Points

It has been a concern from earliest railway times that vehicles, usually goods wagons, have moved out of sidings or loops due to gravity or strong winds. In addition there have been cases where drivers have misread signals whilst in a loop or siding and headed for the main line whilst another train was approaching on it.

The trap point is a device that will deliberately derail a train whose driver has passed a signal at danger whilst on a loop line, thus preventing a far more serious accident involving a collision with another train on the main line.

The trap and catch points illustrated in Figs 66 and 67 are at Woofferton Junction near Ludlow.

In Fig. 66 the facing trap point is on the loop line on the left of the picture, near the W16 signal post, and is of the single-rail type. The up line to Shrewsbury is on the left and runs to the top of the picture. The down to Hereford is on the far right and runs to the bottom of the picture.

This means that only one rail is switched to derail a runaway train or wagon. There are versions where both rails are switched.

Fig. 66 Trap point at the end of a loop at Woofferton Junction near Ludlow, August 2014.

These trap points move in concert with the point that controls the exit onto the main line. All of this is interlocked with the signals.

In 1940 the GWR suffered one of its worst accidents when a driver misread signals at night for the track he was on and plunged off the end of trap points at Norton Fitzwarren near Taunton in Somerset. Twenty-seven people lost their lives but at the official enquiry it was judged that the consequences would have been much worse if the train had been allowed to crash into another train on an adjacent track.

Catch Points

These trailing points are usually spring-loaded to the derail position and are there to derail a vehicle that has run back along a running line in the opposite direction to the normal running direction. They used to be common on running lines and were one of the reasons why wrong line running could be problematic. All main line railway rolling stock is now fitted with automatically acting brakes, rather than the type that had to be manually applied, and so the need for catch points has been reduced.

Fig. 67 depicts a set of catch points at the entrance to the up goods loop at Woofferton Junction. The catch points are to the right of the ground disc.

If a train needed to be reversed out of the loop, the catch points would need to be closed first.

Track Circuiting

In the nineteenth and twentieth centuries there were accidents caused by signallers forgetting the presence of a train in their section, particularly where the service was intensive, so a track circuit was devised that could detect the presence of a train in a section.

Fig. 67 Catch point at the other end of the goods loop at Woofferton Junction, August 2014.

LINESIDE SIGNALLING EQUIPMENT

In the drawing in Fig. 68 the track is electrically split into sections that tally with operational needs, usually to do with running line speed. A low-voltage current is passed through both rails and this is fed to a relay coil. A relay is an electrical switch that can have many sets of contacts and is changed over when the coil is energized. Relays are remote-controlled switches.

When no vehicle is present the relay is held energized and this holds off any indication that the track circuit is occupied.

Fig. 69 shows what happens when a vehicle wheel is detected in the section shown. The battery supply is short-circuited and the relay drops out to give a Track Occupied indication. It is not a dead short circuit as there is a shunt resistor in the circuit, which is not shown.

The relay is normally energized when there is no vehicle present so that the system is failsafe. If the battery fails or the wiring is faulty or the relay coil burns out, a safe 'track occupied' indication will be given.

Originally this track circuiting lit a lamp on a diagram, but later provided an electro-mechanical lock so that a signaller could not pull off signals for a section unless that track circuit was clear of traffic.

The railway rulebooks (rule 55) required drivers to telephone the signaller to alert them to their presence when halted at a signal. Most signals now have a lozenge-shaped plaque or painted-on indicator on the signal or ground disc and this tells the train driver that the track is track circuited. As such, there is then no requirement to telephone under rule 55. The more modern version would be to exchange SMS messages on the GSM-R system. This is a system adapted from mobile phone technology specifically for railways.

With the introduction of extremely long lengths of continuously welded rail, the original DC battery system has been supplanted by a system based around an alternating current circuit that relies on identifying a voltage of a different frequency relating to a specific section of track.

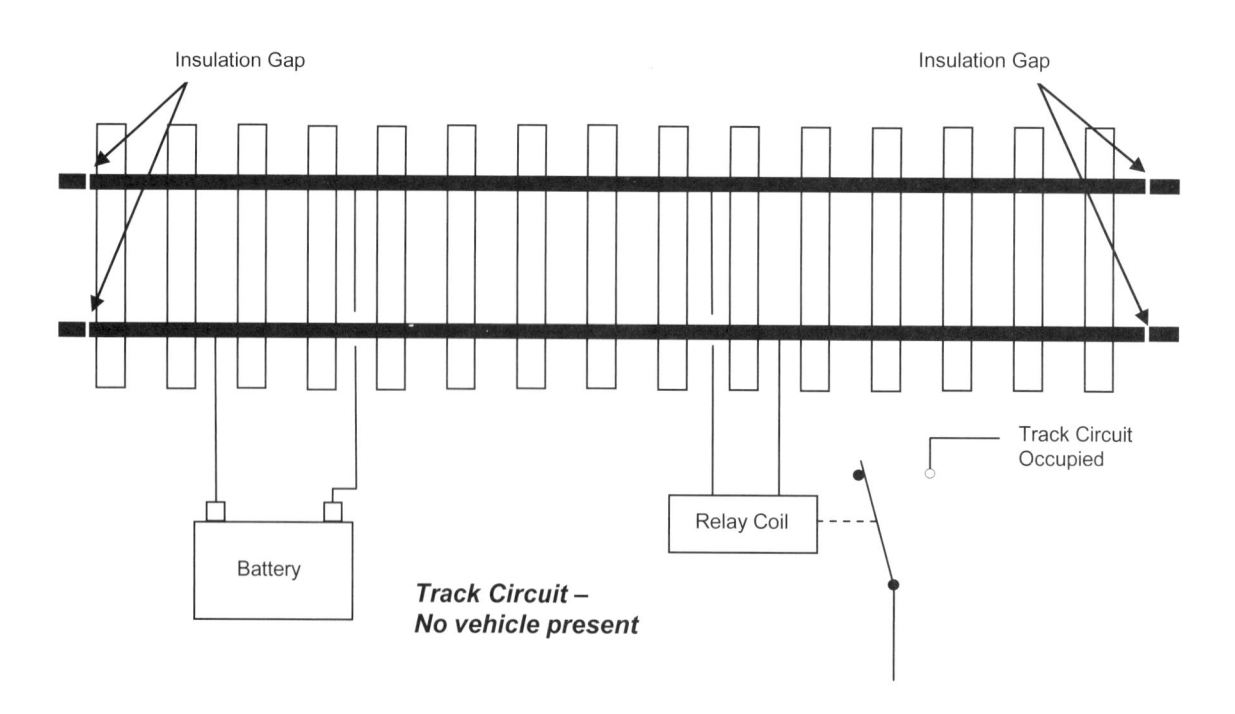

Fig. 68 Diagram of a simplified track circuit showing 'track unoccupied'.

LINESIDE SIGNALLING EQUIPMENT

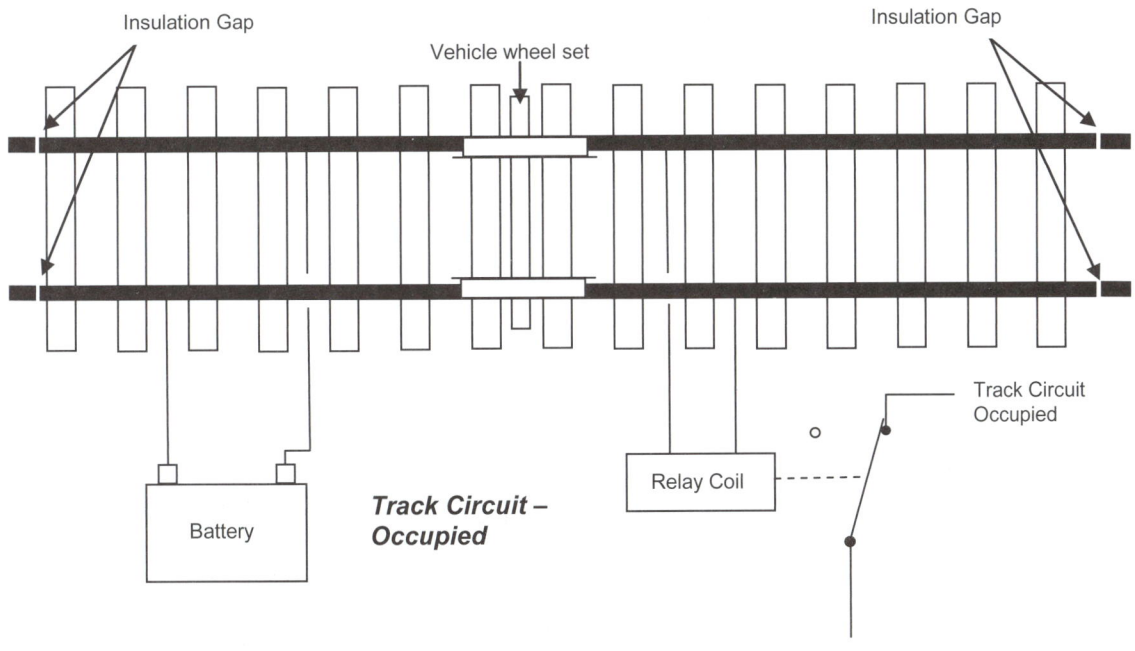

Fig. 69 Diagram of a simplified track circuit showing 'track occupied'.

Fig. 70 depicts a collection of track-circuited signals with the white-painted lozenge shape on the signal posts. These signals are at Park Junction, Newport in South Wales.

Berth Track Circuit

There are numerous references to this term in other signalling-related media and it simply means the track circuit that a train is standing on when it has been brought to a stand at a home signal.

Fig. 70 A collection of track-circuited signals at Park Junction Newport, South Wales, August 2006.

Automatic Warning System (AWS)

The origins of this go back to 1905 and the Great Western Railway's Automatic Train Control (ATC) system. This system used a ramp placed near to a distant signal that gave an audible bell sound if passing the distant signal at OFF or clear.

If the signal was ON or at danger, there would be a different audible horn warning and a visual one too. In addition, under a signal ON condition the train's brakes would operate unless the train driver cancelled the operation by acknowledging the alarm. Clearly these warnings of passing distant signals whether OFF or ON were a boon in fog or falling snow, where visibility was much reduced.

The GWR system relied on contacts between locomotives and ramps between the tracks. In the 1930s a private firm developed a further system that relied on an induced voltage without direct contact, much in the same way as in an electrical transformer.

The successor to the latter system is in operation today. An inoperative AWS system fitted to a power car on an InterCity 125 locomotive was adjudged to be partially responsible for the Southall rail crash in September 1997, where seven people died and many were injured. Signals passed at danger (SPADs) were also involved, but this was thought to be due to the inoperative AWS. Had the AWS been operative it is thought that the train driver would have reacted to signals passed first at caution and then at danger as he would have had the audible alarm reminder.

Train Protection and Warning System (TPWS) takes this form of automation a stage further and is being progressively fitted to the Network Rail system. It is more of a control than a warning system.

Fig. 71 shows a modern inductor-type AWS ramp at the former GWR station at Wrexham General.

Fig. 71   AWS inductor ramp at Wrexham General station, August 2014.

CHAPTER 2

Ways of Working

Absolute Block – AB

Originally there was the time interval system, which meant you could dispatch a train some minutes after the passage of another. This was all well and good until the original train was stopped for some reason or traffic densities and speeds increased.

A concept used almost since railways began is the 'block' of track, where a train is permitted to move from block to block provided no other train is in the block being moved to. This relies on there being up and down tracks. Single lines have their own arrangements and will be covered later in the book. It is usual to consider trains travelling in the up direction to be heading towards London, but there are local variations.

This block system was worked by block instruments that conveyed the track occupancy status and by a bell system that was used to communicate with adjacent signal boxes.

If you look at Fig. 72 you can see the GWR 1947 absolute block instrument together with the block

Fig. 72 The block shelf at Norton Junction signal box near Worcester depicting instruments to communicate with Worcester Shrub Hill signal box, November 2005.

Fig. 73 GWR 1947 block instrument, now the mainstay of AB working signal boxes, from the author's collection, August 2014.

bell on the right. This is the means of dealing with trains to and from Worcester Shrub Hill and Norton Junction signal box, which is where the photograph was taken. The block bell is a single-strike instrument, which means when you press the key on the front once, the corresponding bell at Worcester Shrub Hill rings once. Conversely pressing the key once at Worcester Shrub Hill once would ring the bell here at Norton Junction once.

The default condition for the section of track is described as Normal, which means the same as Line Blocked. In other words, no permissions have been granted for any movement.

Fig. 73 gives a close-up view of a GWR 1947 block instrument.

The sector to the left, coloured green, is Line Clear, and this cannot be selected until the button beneath the dial is pushed and the handle rotated clockwise. The sector to the right is Train on Line, and that is coloured red.

This instrument on the block shelf at Norton Junction controls the up line and the upper dial indicator is a repeater from Worcester Shrub Hill of what the signaller there has selected for the line down to Norton Junction. It is quite possible to have both dials showing something, as the trains are on separate lines.

Fig. 74 is a representation at a most basic level of the structure of a block section. Network Rail actual locations may be different for mainly operational reasons and there may well be more signals in the sections at busier parts of the railway.

Under consideration is a train passing on the up line from signal box A to signal box B, from the point of view of the train driver. Certain terms describe the relative positions of these boxes. After the train passes box A, this signal box is said to be 'in the rear of' and signal box B 'in advance of' the train until the train passes it.

The table opposite outlines the communication between the two signal boxes to pass an express passenger train from box A to box B.

Absolute Block Working

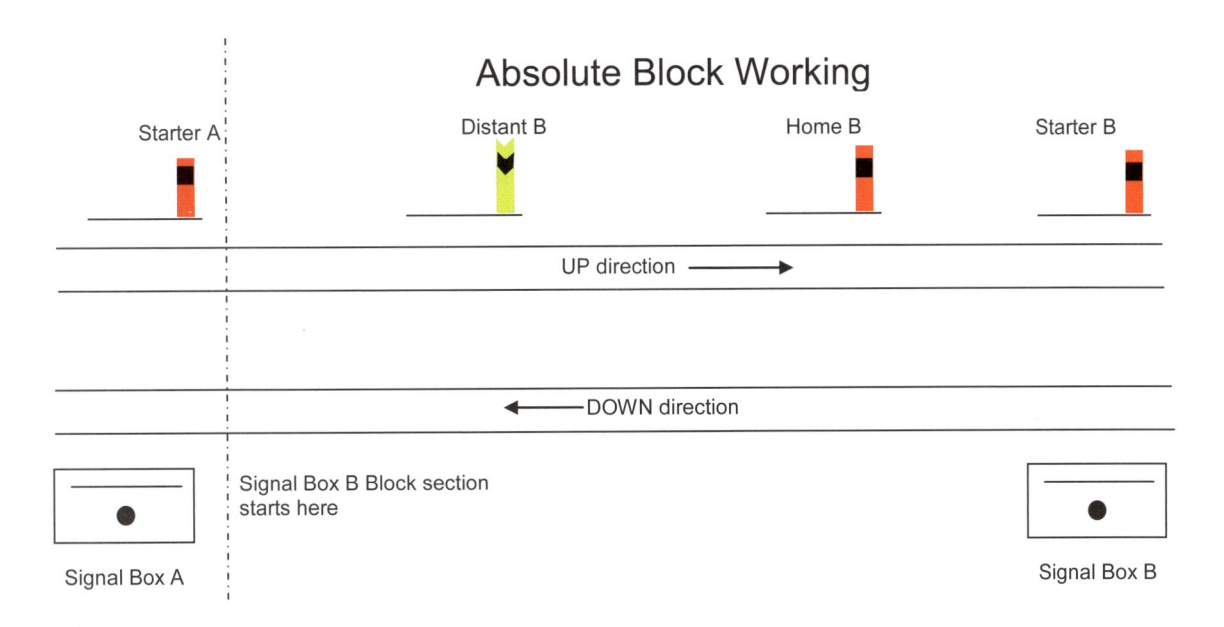

Fig. 74 A simplified representation of block sections between two signal boxes. The signals on the up side would be mirrored on the down side but are omitted for the sake of clarity.

Signal Box A			Signal Box B		
Bell	**Meaning**	**Instrument**	**Bell**	**Meaning**	**Instrument**
1	Call Attention	Normal	1	Attending	Normal
4	Line Clear for express?	Normal	4	Line is clear for express	Line Clear **selected**
	Reflects on up line dial	Line Clear			Line Clear
2	Train entering section	Line Clear	2	Acknowledge train entering section	Train on Line **selected**
	Reflects on up line dial	Train on Line			Train on Line
		Train on Line	2.1	Train out of section	Train on Line
2.1	Acknowledge train out of section	Train on Line			Normal **selected**
	Reflects on up line dial	Normal			Normal

When signal box B selects Line Clear, the signaller at box A can clear A's section signals to allow the train to enter section A. Otherwise a train might overrun into B, where there might be an obstruction. Similarly, B cannot clear section B's signals until Line Clear has been received from the next up signal box. Signal box A sends two bells when the train has passed starter A.

Train out of Section

The train out of section is confirmation from box B to A that the train has passed through B complete with a tail lamp. This signifies that the train is complete. A vehicle left in a section could also be detected by a track circuit but a more definite method is the use of axle counters, which are more common in areas controlled by track circuit blocks, (*see* Track Circuit Block section below). CCTV cameras are commonly used where it is not possible for the signaller to view the rear of a train for train out of section purposes. Such an installation can be found at Droitwich Spa.

Clearing Point

In addition, before a signaller can clear signals for a section, the clearing point must also be clear. A clearing point is a position at least a quarter mile past the starter signal and can be thought of as a margin of safety. The clearing point is covered in the next section.

Should it be necessary to bring a train to a stand at a starter signal, the clearing point is a notional space to allow the train to overrun the signal without imminent danger to a train in the next section.

Bell Codes

The bell codes encountered so far are not even a scratch on the surface of the system of codes built up over the years, reflecting the complexity of types of trains being run together with many ancillary message codes for either routine or emergency purposes.

Train Register

Every bell code sent or received has to be recorded with the time in the train register in manuscript. In earlier days a precision clock was provided by the signal works at Reading for just this purpose. Many of the clocks came from Kay's of Worcester.

This serves as a record of train movements and is immediately impounded if there is any accident or mishap. A more modern version of this would be a flight data recorder on a commercial airliner. Train event recorders have been around for some years. When signalling data is received in the cabs of all trains, event recorders will be compulsory.

All of this is for one train on one section in one direction – each signal box has both up and down sections and each signal box has at least two sets of instruments unless it is at a terminus station. Signal boxes that are junctions or quadruple tracked will have many sets of block instruments. Block instruments are interlocked with signals and track circuits to provide a very safe system that can only really be defeated by a deliberate act.

Intermediate Block Section – IBS

Rather than a painful abdominal condition, in railway signalling terms an IBS is where a block section has been split into two to enable a more densely packed traffic pattern to be handled. In the days of freight trains that could only average 10–15mph (16–24km/h), section occupation for long periods could be a real problem. They are not so common now. There is an example of an IBS at Par signal box in Cornwall (*see* Fig. 322).

Track Circuit Block – TCB

Track circuit block is really all to do with colour light signals, which, strictly speaking are outside the scope of this book, except that many signal boxes interface with track circuit block sections and will have track circuit block equipment or indications in them.

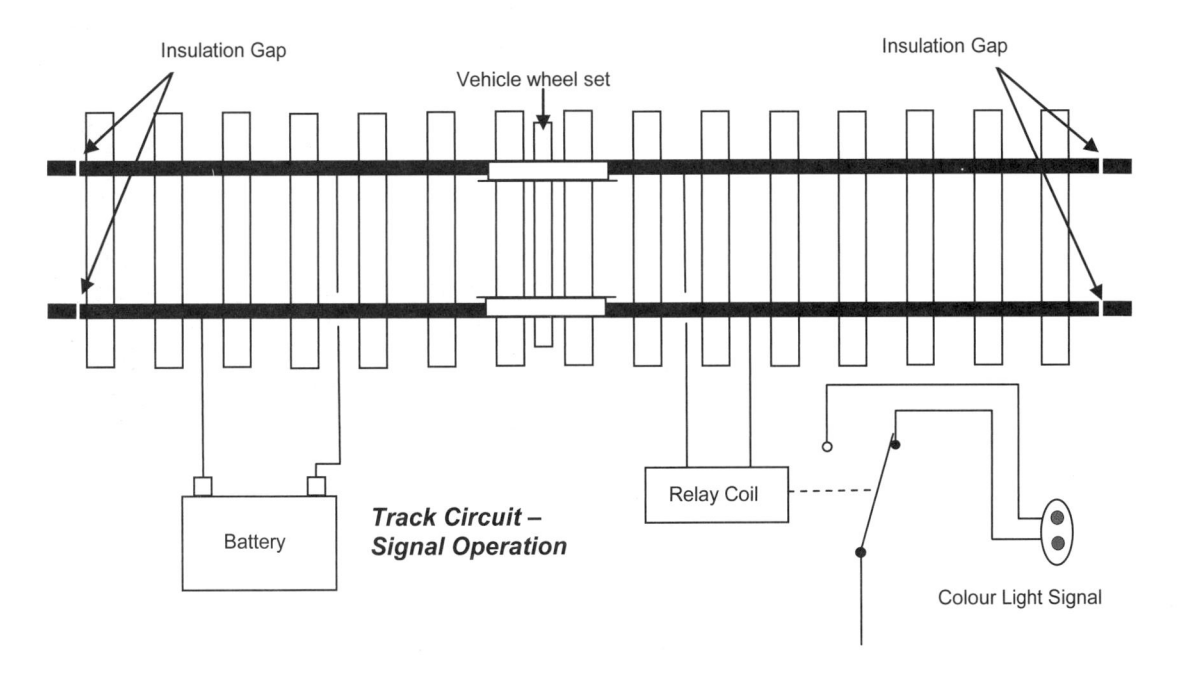

Fig. 75 A basic drawing of a track circuit controlling a colour light signal using a DC power supply. More usually now, because of continuously welded rail sections of track, the unit works on AC with differing frequency circuits.

Originally track circuits lit a lamp in a signal box to indicate where a train was. Then they were used to interlock block instruments, signals and points to provide a safe working semaphore signal environment.

With colour light signals it is possible to provide automatically changing signals that are controlled by the passage of trains or presence of vehicles on the track.

The simplified diagram in Fig. 75 illustrates the principle, but the reality is more complicated in the sense that colour light signals can display up to four aspects (or more if flashing colour lights are included). These additional aspects have been employed on track with high line speeds.

The indications of a multiple-aspect signal are:

Red Must not be passed at all
Double yellow Can be passed but expect caution at next signal
Yellow Caution – expect next signal to be at danger
Green Proceed

TCB is primarily used on double up and down lines but can be used on some single lines. In the event of a train coming to a halt unexpectedly in a section, it is the guard's responsibility to protect the rear of the train by placing a shorting clip in the section beyond the one in which the train is standing. In TCB territory this would place preceding signals to danger. Network Rail term the clip a TCOD (track circuit operating device). The guard is also obliged to put down explosive detonators on the track at a considerable distance from an unexpectedly halted train, which act as an audible alarm to a following train.

Single-Line Working

Both absolute block and track circuit block are either wholly or almost always concerned with double line up and down working. Single lines need special arrangements.

Single lines rely on either a token or a signed pass, termed a ticket, or a combination of the two. The token has to be in the possession of the driver before the train can proceed along a single line. The action of issuing the driver with a token locks the issue of a token for the same section in the opposite direction. It is the driver's responsibility to check that the correct token for the line being travelled has been issued. It is the signaller's responsibility to ensure that the driver is issued with the token for that section of line being travelled. The Abermule disaster in 1921 was the result of a driver being handed the wrong token and then proceeding with it.

Key Token – KT

This system consists of an electrically locked token instrument at both ends of a section of single line.

Fig. 76 depicts key tokens in the instrument at Goonbarrow Junction in Cornwall. Key token is worked from there to St Blazey signal box.

A token request by signal box A is made to the opposite end of the section being travelled, say signal box B. The signaller at B presses a release, which enables a token at A to be taken out of the machine and handed to the driver. The token machine is now locked at B. The driver, who also has to obey all signals, has the authority to proceed to B, where the token for that section must be surrendered before a fresh token can be issued to proceed further along the line. The token is often encased in a leather pouch and attached to a hoop apparatus to enable it to be hooked around the driver's or signaller's arm. Fig. 77 shows the key token apparatus complete with keys at Goonbarrow Junction, Cornwall.

Fig. 76 Key tokens in the instrument at Goonbarrow Junction signal box, October 2004.

No Signaller Key Token – NSKT

This is a little misleading in that a signaller issues a token for a single line but the operation of the instrument at the other end of the section is by a train driver. This is only suitable for lightly used lines.

No Signaller Key Token Remote – NSKTR

This is where a signaller issues a token at both ends of a line. The train driver then operates a succession of token exchanges at passing loops on the single line. This slows down the process but enables a line to be run with only one signaller at each end. It is also only suitable for lightly trafficked lines.

Such a line is the Central Wales line that runs from Craven Arms in Shropshire to Pantyffynnon in Carmarthenshire in West Wales. In the event of a failure of the token apparatus drivers can be issued with a written authority to proceed.

One Train Staff – OTS

Here a single train is issued with a staff or token to proceed. Once that staff for that section of track has been issued no further trains can enter that section. There is an override in case a train breaks down in a section but that will be under strict rules and regulations. This type of working is typically

Fig. 77 Key token instrument at Goonbarrow Junction signal box, October 2004.

found where there is a single line with no sidings or loops. Quite often a branch line that terminates in a single platform, such as Newquay, uses this system. If loco-hauled stock are required to use these lines then 'top and tail' working with an engine at both ends is needed.

Tokenless Block – TB

As its name implies, there is no token exchange with these lines in an attempt to speed up the process of single-line working. It works by interlocking signals that could signal a conflicting move along the single line and requires special block instruments. This system is found on the Worcester to Hereford section.

Train Staff and Ticket – TS&T

Train staff and ticket is where a token, ticket or signed pass is issued to a train driver by a signaller. Authority to proceed is also by section signal admission.

ERTMS

This is the European Rail Traffic Management System, which brings control into the train cab and works together with GSM-R mobile phone voice communication between signaller and train driver. This system is in use on the Cambrian lines, but is expected to be rolled out network-wide.

CHAPTER 3

Signal Boxes and Infrastructure on Network Rail

This survey was carried out between 2003 and 2014 and represents a wide cross-section of the remaining signal boxes on Network Rail. Inevitably some have closed and been demolished. If you are intending visiting any of them it is suggested that you find out what the current status is before you set off.

For reasons of access and position some signal boxes are covered in greater detail than others and some are featured as a 'focus on' where the quality of the information or the interest of that location merits the attention.

The survey is presented by area wherever possible although some are inevitably on their own as they are the last survivors locally.

Some of the signal boxes have been reduced in status over the years and whilst they may have controlled block sections in the past some no longer do so but are (or were at the time of the survey) on Network Rail's payroll as working signal boxes.

Details of the numbers of levers are included but not all the levers may be fully functional as signal boxes have been constantly modified over the years.

Lever colours are:

Red	Home signals
Yellow	Distant signals
Black	Points
Blue	Facing point locks
Blue/brown	Wicket gates at level crossings
Black/Yellow chevrons	Detonator placers
White	Not in use

Levers under the block shelf or towards the front window are said to be normal, and those pulled over to the rear of the box are said to be reversed.

Listed Buildings

Many signal boxes are considered to have architectural or historic merit and are Grade II listed by English Heritage or CADW. This basically means they cannot be changed externally without permission. If the owner allows the building to decay to such an extent that it is unsafe, the building can then be demolished. The number of signal boxes with a listing is due to increase on the news that they are all to be replaced by 2020.

Signal Box Official Abbreviation

Every signal box on Network Rail has an official abbreviation of one, two or sometimes three letters.

This appears on all signal posts relevant to that box. Finding an abbreviation can be tricky, as there are eight signal boxes with Norton in the title, for example, until you realize that they are not unique. The abbreviation for each box appears after the box title in this book, if it has one.

Summary of Disposition

The lines that were mainly semaphore signalled when surveyed are:

Gobowen – Shrewsbury – Hereford – Newport
Hereford – Worcester – Cotswold Line to Ascott-under-Wychwood, Oxfordshire
Cornwall – main line, Liskeard to Penzance and Newquay Branch
Chester – Wolverhampton
North Warwickshire line

Other areas that were sporadically semaphore signalled or retained former mechanical signal boxes:

Cambrian Coast
South Wales
West Wales

Together with odd representatives from:

Bristol area
Gloucestershire
Banbury, Oxfordshire
West London
Yeovil Pen Mill, Somerset

This does not claim to be an all-encompassing list and there are odd stragglers that were not surveyed and are now no more.

Worcester Area

Fig. 78 shows the arrangement of the lines around Worcester, with the signal boxes appearing as black discs. Worcester Shrub Hill station is not shown separately as it is co-located with the signal box.

Fairly large junctions away from major cities tend to survive longer as semaphore signalling centres, as the costs of modernization seem to outweigh the operational benefits as traffic volumes would not generate sufficient revenue to justify the expense – at least until recent years.

Worcester is a fine city steeped in history and with a venerated cathedral. As well as being a place

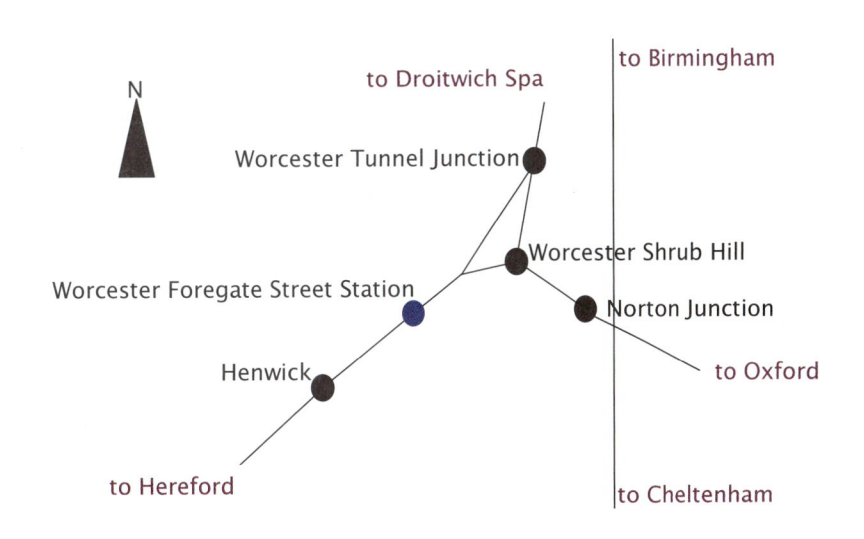

Fig. 78 A schematic drawing of signal boxes and their connections in the Worcester area.

of interest historically, it also provided employment at Kay's, who were early watch and clock makers to the GWR, latterly a catalogue firm; and Mackenzie and Holland, who supplied signalling equipment in early years. This is the original home of the famous Worcestershire sauce, while Royal Worcester porcelain has been synonymous with the highest-quality hand-painted wares from as early as the eighteenth century.

An original railway in the area in the 1850s was the Oxford, Worcester and Wolverhampton Railway, which, according to popular opinion at the time, was truly shocking. It was known deprecatingly as the Old Worse and Worse. It was taken over, after a sub-amalgamation, by the GWR in 1863 and yet you can still see railway property in Droitwich Spa, notably bridges, with the OWW initials. The old name lives on.

This is also a joint line area in that the GWR and the LMS (formerly Midland Railway) had a significant presence in the area. The line running north–south in Fig. 78 from Birmingham to Cheltenham is the former Midland Railway (LMS) main line.

Worcester also contains much of the unusual and rare signalling items that can still (in 2014) be found on Network Rail. It is distinctive operationally in that it has two stations – at Shrub Hill and Foregate Street – due to the way the junctions are arranged. Both stations are of interest architecturally and are substantially original.

For many years the GWR ran the Cathedrals Express to Oxford, Worcester and Hereford and that train runs to this day. In 1957 the Western Region renamed a Castle class locomotive to be 7005, Sir Edward Elgar, after the famous composer who lived in the Malvern Hills nearby, and 7005 was a Worcester engine all its life.

Imported coal is unloaded at Portbury Docks near Bristol, and the Worcester area sees some freight traffic from here to the West Midlands and Rugeley power station. DRS route some nuclear flask reprocessing trains from Hinkley Point power station in Somerset via Worcester on their way to Sellafield in Cumbria. There is other freight traffic of an irregular nature.

Worcester Shrub Hill (SH)

Date Built	1935
GWR Type or Builder	GWR 11+
No. of Levers	84
Ways of Working	AB, TCB
Current Status	Active
Listed (Y/N)	N

Shrub Hill station, which this signal box controls, started life as a classic through station with two main platforms for up and down trains, a loop line for secondary or parcels trains and terminus platforms, called bays, for branch line trains. There was another signal box at Wyld's Lane Junction, in the Oxford direction, within sight of Shrub Hill signal box and another signal box in the goods sidings behind the station.

The late 1960s and 1970s saw loss of traffic on both passenger and freight services, caused by increased car ownership and the collapse of coal traffic with the end of steam traction and move towards centrally heated homes rather than coal fires.

In November 1973 the area was rationalized or cut back and the closure of Wyld's Lane signal box meant Shrub Hill had to take on the work with remotely powered points. As another consequence of the Wyld's Lane closure, the freight through roads behind the station are controlled by the North Sidings Ground Frame, which is released or overseen by Shrub Hill box.

The area was resignalled to enable two-way running on what had been the up and down main lines.

Shrub Hill works TCB to Tunnel Junction signal box and AB to Henwick and Norton Junction. Oddly, though, Tunnel Junction works to Shrub Hill by AB!

There have been schemes, notably in the 1990s, to further rationalize and modernize the Worcester area but these have not been implemented.

The signal box depicted in Fig. 79 has an internal staircase and bricked-up locking frame windows. This was a common change in World War II to prevent the blast from aerial bombing damaging the locking frame on the ground floor. The windows

Fig. 79   Worcester Shrub Hill Station signal box, July 2014.

are UPVC replacements and tend to change the character of the building. The iron rods outside the windows are original and are for signallers to lean on to chat to drivers and other people, although ostensibly they appear to have a health and safety function.

In view of the number of images depicting Shrub Hill for various reasons previously, only Fig. 80 is offered for study here.

The building on the right is a former goods shed and it still bears a Great Western Railway painted sign although the building has passed into other uses. The sidings controlled by the North Sidings Ground Frame are on the left, somewhat overgrown, and what had been the loop platform line, and is now a siding, is seen towards the centre of the picture. The main running line to the right of the passenger siding is protected from it by a double-railed trap point. The signal in the distance is the down home from Norton Junction with calling on arm. Wyld's Lane Junction, where the freight lines rejoin the main line, is in the distance.

Fig. 81 just shows Shrub Hill signal box's relative position to the station. The view is towards Oxford.

Fig. 80   Worcester Shrub Hill station looking towards the Oxford line, November 2008. Note the double-bladed trap point and freight loops on the left.

Fig. 81   Worcester Shrub Hill station itself with the signal box at the end of the opposite platform, November 2008.

Worcester Tunnel Junction (TJ)

Date Built	1905
GWR Type or Builder	GWR 7
No. of Levers	58
Ways of Working	AB, TCB
Current Status	Active
Listed (Y/N)	N

Just over half a mile (1km) from Shrub Hill station signal box is Tunnel Junction. It controls the through freight sidings past Shrub Hill station, the loco depot sidings and the route towards Birmingham via Droitwich Spa. There is also a route from Hereford and Foregate Street station to Droitwich Spa.

As with the whole network, the signal box's work and equipment have reduced over years: it started life with seventy-seven levers and is now reduced to fifty-eight.

Fig. 82 is a general view showing the same revamped windows as Shrub Hill but no ventilator cowls, which are an original feature. What the building does have, however, is a splendid cast iron name plate, which is most definitely original. Also in the original style are the wooden steps up to the operating floor. The locking frame window apertures have been bricked up but the one on the far left has been rebuilt, as has that end of the box. To the left of the box is the end of one of the loco sidings, and one day in the 1970s a train driver misread a signal and drove the train through the buffer stops and into the signal box. Unfortunately the attractive end corners in engineer's blue brick were not restored. That would have been a requirement had the box been listed.

The box works AB to Shrub Hill and TCB from Shrub Hill, AB to Henwick and AB to Droitwich Spa. There is a fourth set of block instruments for the through freight line past Shrub Hill station.

Fig. 83 illustrates that the point rodding and signal wires for the manually operated equipment can be routed to the rear of a box as well as traditionally at the front. In a junction situation it makes more economic sense.

The signal box, like many other larger buildings, had a coal fireplace, and the remains of the chimney stack are visible.

The reason for the Tunnel part of the name is clear with Rainbow Hill Tunnel in the background. A train is signalled out of Shrub Hill to go towards Droitwich. The lines on the left are from Worcester Foregate Street station and Hereford via the Malverns.

Fig. 84 is the signalling diagram for Tunnel Junction box. There is a list at the top of unused levers. Then on the diagram itself you can see the lines from Droitwich Spa on the left, following through to Shrub Hill on the right, and above those lines the through freight roads. Below the Shrub Hill lines are the locomotive depot tracks in light blue and below that the line from Foregate Street station. The numbers of signals that are on the diagram correspond to numbers plated on the actual signal posts. The red block on the left of the tunnel is a limit of shunt indicator for a train driver. The black oval-shaped figures on the black tracks are track circuit indicators. You can see that the freight roads and the loco sidings are not track circuited, so signals in those areas do not have the lozenge shape on the front.

Fig. 82 Worcester Tunnel Junction signal box, July 2014. Note the rebuilt brickwork on the left, the result of a train hitting the signal box.

Fig. 85 is part of the block shelf at Tunnel Junction. The upper dial on the block instrument on the left for Droitwich Spa is Droitwich telling Tunnel Junction it is ready, with Line Clear, for the train being sent to Droitwich.

The Shrub Hill block instrument has its Shrub Hill AB indicator thoughtfully replaced with a GWR steam express picture, as Shrub Hill works TCB to Tunnel Junction.

The black Bakelite round items with brass knobs on are plungers that release electrical locks. The locking frame is below the operating floor and locks can be mechanical or electrical. Levers that were originally designed to operate rods or wires sometimes operate switches – distant signals are a case in point if they have been converted to colour light signals.

The red annular gadgets hanging on the hook below the shelf are signal lever collars. They are used to remind signallers usually of the presence of a train at their signal. The Hawes Junction disaster of 1910 on the Settle to Carlisle route of the Midland Railway was ascribed to a signaller forgetting the presence of light engines at a signal, although the driver should have obeyed rule 55 and reminded the signaller the locomotive was there. All this was before track circuiting.

These are not used much now that most of the lines are track circuited, but might be used with freights in the through roads or locos leaving the depot.

The brass-faced rectangular box with the winding handle on top is a Welwyn Release. Like so many safety devices in signal boxes, they have their origins in a railway accident. In 1935 on the LNER at Welwyn Garden City station a signaller there accepted a train into a section at night that was already occupied by a train. The resulting collision killed fourteen people and injured twenty-nine. The outcome of this was the Welwyn Control, where track circuits were employed and these were interlocked not only with signals but with block instruments as well. This made it impossible to accept a train – give Line Clear – when there was a train already in the section.

Fig. 83 Worcester Tunnel Junction signal box looking towards Rainbow Hill tunnel, March 2008.

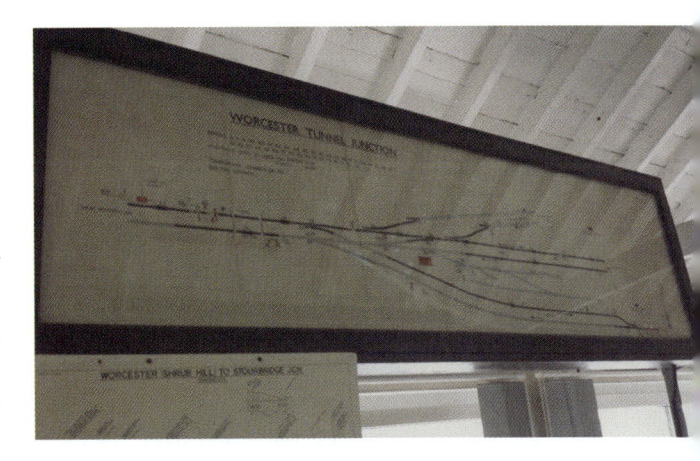

Fig. 84 Worcester Tunnel Junction signal box diagram showing track-circuited lines in black and other lines in light blue, July 2014.

Fig. 85 Worcester Tunnel Junction signal box with a fine selection of block instruments on the shelf, July 2014. Note the different-shaped bells to give different ring tones

Fig. 86 Worcester Tunnel Junction signal box lever frame with four of the levers reversed, July 2014.

The release is a manual control that overrides the locking of the block instruments but still introduces a time delay to ensure nothing happens without due care and attention.

On to Fig. 86 now, and this shows the levers in their frame. The yellow lever at the end is a colour light signal and so only operates a switch connected to the lever. The levers have ivorine plates fitted underneath the handles and these are to describe the order in which levers are pulled, due to the interlocks present. You can't pull off signals if the points for that route are not set properly, and before facing points can be pulled over the locks have to be withdrawn and so on.

The four block bells can be seen and each one has a different-shaped bell so that the signaller can tell which line is active by the tone of the ring. There is one bell for each passenger route and one for the through freight loop.

The other essential piece of equipment is the signaller's armchair.

Outside the box again, this time looking back towards Shrub Hill station (Fig. 87). Of the two signals in the middle of the picture, the larger one is the down home signal for Droitwich (TJ17) and the smaller one to the right is the loco yard exit signal (TJ39). It was these two signals that the driver in the 1970s confused, as related above under Fig. 82. Apparently he mistook the TJ17 for the loco yard exit and ended up going through the buffer stops and into the signal box. They are together because of sighting reasons but it should have been clear from the size of the arm and lack of track circuit which was the loco yard signal.

Fig. 88 is an image of another fairly rare piece of kit nowadays – the GWR-style point lever in the loco yard. Points that do not have a running line connection are usually hand operated using hand signals between driver and shunter. In GWR days there would have been a white-painted guard rail for safety.

Fig. 87 Worcester Tunnel Junction from the top of the signal box steps, with, from left to right, lines to Goods avoiding loops, Shrub Hill station, Foregate Street station and Hereford, July 2014. The signals referred to in the text are almost in the dead centre of the picture.

Fig. 88   GWR-type manually operated point lever in the loco yard at Worcester Tunnel Junction, April 2005.

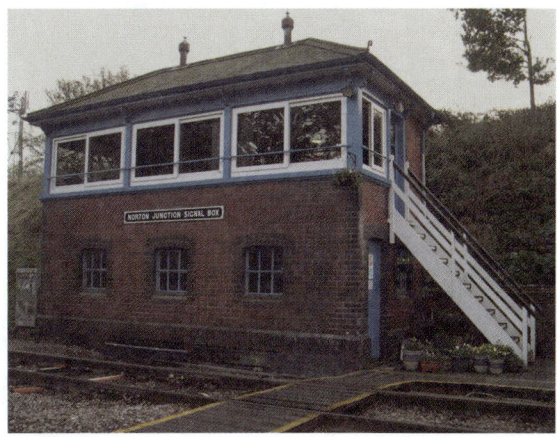

Fig. 89   Norton Tunnel Junction signal box near Worcester. Winter flowering pansies are in bloom, November 2005.

Norton Junction (NJ)

Date Built	1908
GWR Type or Builder	GWR 7
No. of Levers	19
Ways of Working	AB, TCB, KT
Current Status	Active
Listed (Y/N)	N

Norton Junction is where the line to Oxford and Paddington intersects the former Midland main line from Birmingham to Cheltenham. The box works AB to Worcester Shrub Hill, TCB to Gloucester power box and KT to Evesham on the Cotswold line towards Oxford.

Fig. 89 introduces another feature of more rural signal boxes – flowers and cultivation. The box, windows apart, is delightfully original with cast iron name plate, roof cowl ventilators, locking frame windows and wooden staircase. The boarded walkway has been provided to issue or pick up the single line token to or from Evesham.

In Fig. 90, the diagram clearly shows that the single track to Evesham and Worcester is the main line, as this was GWR, and the double-track line to the right is the branch, as this was Midland Railway territory. The junction at Abbot's Wood is a little way off from the signal box. The GWR Cotswold line crosses over the top of the Midland line.

Fig. 91, still at Norton Junction, shows the lever frame with a few levers reversed. The signaller's duster is just visible and this is necessary as the

Fig. 90   Norton Tunnel Junction signal box diagram, November 2005. Note the single track is main (GWR) and the double track after the junction is branch (Midland Railway). To the left the diagram would have said Wyld's Lane Junction but now says Shrub Hill.

57

Fig. 91 Norton Tunnel Junction signal box lever frame with spider plants to brighten the place up a bit, November 2005.

levers are plain steel. The moisture from hands would make the lever tops rusty over time so a cloth is needed. (The lever handles are also polished in many boxes. In fact, a bit of pride in the appearance of the box is a tradition that goes way back.) Brasses and brown linoleum polished are still to be seen. The brown linoleum, or lino, is making way for thermoplastic floor coverings and the like.

Fig. 92 shows a fine set of block instruments on the shelf with polished brass bits. The Worcester-labelled instruments are for Shrub Hill while the Evesham block bell is on its own because it is a single line and has the red key token apparatus. Some KT instruments incorporate their own block bell in the token housing but not this one apparently. The small rotary device with the handle is a

Fig. 92 Norton Tunnel Junction signal box block shelf. The pride in appearance and pride in the job show up well here, November 2005.

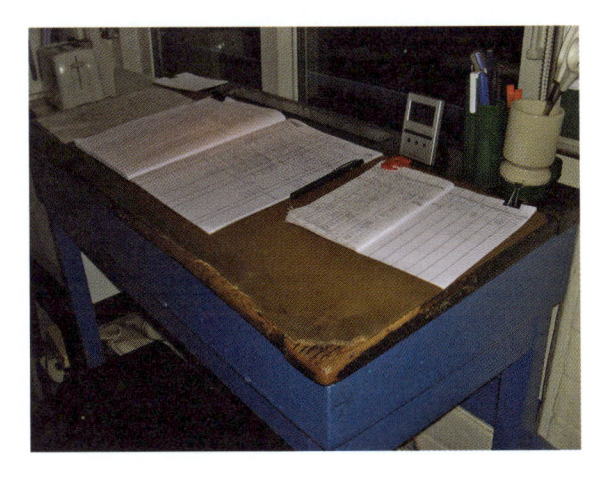

Fig. 93 Norton Tunnel Junction signal box train register and original desk, November 2005.

Fig. 94 Henwick signal box, March 2005.

more modern form of Welwyn Control release that we first saw at Tunnel Junction. The black rectangular devices next to the Welwyn release are 'lever locked by track circuit' indicators.

The lamp next to Evesham's block bell is a 'Bardic' lamp and as well as being a torch is an emergency signalling device in that it can display red and green aspects as well as white. Signallers also have red, green and yellow flags for emergency signalling use.

Finally, Fig. 93 shows the train register and desk. Every bell code sent and received at this signal box is recorded here. Note the remnant of brown floor linoleum as a re-covering material for the desk top.

Henwick (HK)

Date Built	1875 (estimated)
GWR Type or Builder	Mackenzie and Holland Type 1
No. of Levers	25
Ways of Working	AB
Current Status	Active
Listed (Y/N)	N

Henwick is an example of a signal box that has gained status and responsibility over the years.

Originally boxes like Henwick started life as a gate box, that is, controlling a level crossing. As the supervised level-crossing function was still needed when it came for signal boxes to be closed it was seen as cheaper to close larger boxes and transfer the cut-down AB and signalling parts to a former gate box. Now Henwick works AB to Shrub Hill and Tunnel Junction and AB to Newland East signal box on the Hereford line.

It was built by Mackenzie and Holland, who had their signal works at Worcester, in about 1875. The company and its successors disappeared many years ago so the trail goes cold when looking for more accurate information. It has an unmistakable style, and the terracotta finials on the ridge tiles and arched supports on the soffits under the roof eaves have the style of a substantial Victorian house. The signal box was modified by the GWR in 1897.

The rear view of Henwick (Fig. 95) illustrates the chimney stack well enough and but for a chimney pot would be complete. The left-hand finial has lost its terracotta topmost piece. Notice the toilet block tacked on to the left-hand side. In earlier days there were no toilets at most boxes, and as the years went by a chemical toilet in a shed nearby was the norm. This type of toilet survives in use with inland waterways craft.

SIGNAL BOXES AND INFRASTRUCTURE ON NETWORK RAIL

Also in earlier days signal boxes did not have running water or fresh drinking water. It would be delivered by an early morning pick-up goods train that would stop to shunt so would have time to drop off a churn of water daily and collect an empty churn for refilling. Invariably the train crew would be plied with tea.

Foregate Street station is the setting for Fig. 96, and at the end of the platforms you can see the home signals for each line. Both lines are bi-directional here and are signalled as such. Just after the platform is the viaduct over Foregate Street Worcester and after that, after a curve, is Henwick signal box. The view is towards the Hereford line.

Fig. 95 Rear of Henwick signal box showing chimney stack, added toilet block and traffic lookout window, March 2005.

Fig. 96 Foregate Street station looking towards the Hereford line and Henwick signal box, March 2005.

Fig. 97 Henwick signal box looking further down towards Hereford and the crossovers and refuge siding, March 2005.

Back at Henwick box with Fig. 97 and now looking the same way towards the Hereford line and Newland East signal box about 5 miles (8km) further along the line. There is a double crossover further up as well as a refuge siding, hence all the point rodding and signal wires heading that way. The cage is to stop pedestrians and animals being mangled by the barrier-lifting mechanism.

The Cotswold Line

Fig. 98 shows a schematic diagram of the Cotswold line insofar as mechanical signalling is concerned. What it doesn't show is the rich variety of beautiful countryside that the line passes through, from the rich farmland and fruit-growing areas around Pershore and Evesham through to the pleasantly undulating Cotswolds, whose wealth originally came from the wool trade in pre-railway times, to the Thames valley, which has been an artery for trade to London and the Midlands for centuries.

The Cotswold Line is seeing better times after thirty-five years of decline. The main line was converted to single track for much of its length in the 1970s and the train service similarly run down. Some of the line has been restored to double track and the passenger service improved. HST 125 sets are the main source of motive power for express passenger trains, although class 166, class 180 and other diesel multiple units frequent the line.

Freight is scarce on this line except to Honeybourne and the Long Marston depot. Long Marston was a Ministry of Defence establishment; latterly it has housed surplus equipment from the train operating companies. It is the only part of the line in Warwickshire. Honeybourne was the junction for the line from Stratford-upon-Avon to Cheltenham that closed in the 1970s. There were six signal boxes that bore the name Honeybourne in their title. The top of one of them is preserved at Toddington station on the Gloucestershire and Warwickshire Railway.

In 1914 Edward Thomas wrote a poem about Adlestrop and the sleepy ambience of a country station in the height of summer. The station closed in 1966 but the site is close by Moreton-in-Marsh station and the station sign can still be seen in a bus shelter in the village.

After the re-doubling was carried out in 2011, Evesham and Ascott-under-Wychwood had their mechanical signalling removed but this survey predates that situation. The only signal box on the line with semaphore signalling in 2014, at the time of writing, is Moreton-in-Marsh.

Evesham W.R. (E)

Date Built	1957
GWR Type or Builder	British Railways (Western Region)
No. of Levers	42
Ways of Working	KT, AB
Current Status	Active
Listed (Y/N)	N

Fig. 98 The Cotswold Line schematic diagram showing active mechanical signal boxes.

The station at Evesham used to have a Midland Railway station, latterly London Midland Region, complete with goods yard and its own signal box right alongside. There was a connection between the two stations, which is why the signal box is still labelled W.R. for Western Region long after the Midland has been demolished.

Evesham is a major centre for the production of soft fruit and, together with the nearby Pershore station, forwarded massive quantities of fruit to all over Britain. The GWR even had a locomotive named Pershore Plum. There would have been trainloads full of nothing but fruit in special wagons. Road competition and the rise of the supermarket with their diverse acquisition policies eventually reduced this traffic to nothing.

The Midland Railway station closed in 1963 and the track and facilities were cut back. There are now only a couple of sidings at Evesham W.R.

The line from Evesham to Moreton-in-Marsh, singled in the 1970s, was restored to the double-track format in 2011. This has had an effect on the signalling and working. This piece is therefore split into two, with sections on pre–2011 and post–2011.

Up to 2011

Evesham signal box is a replacement for previous structures by British Railways and as such is a distinctly utilitarian building (Fig. 99). Its position at the far end of the passing loop at the station makes for operating difficulties, particularly when it comes to the single-line token.

Usually the train has to stop at the signal box and exchange tokens there. At Evesham this would cause delays to particularly passenger trains and so special arrangements are in place.

On the up side towards Oxford there is a hut just beyond the road overbridge, where an auxiliary token machine is kept. This is operated by the train driver under supervision from the signaller in the box.

On the down side towards Norton Junction there is another auxiliary token machine in the station building and the train driver has access to that. The station building at Evesham is shown in Fig. 100.

In addition to signalling and exchanging tokens the signaller also has to supervise the working of several level crossings, mostly accommodation crossings allowing farmers to cross to fields on the other side of the line.

Up to 1981, Littleton and Badsey crossing was worked by its own crossing keeper, a cottage being provided as a home. Crossing gates had to be opened and closed by the keeper as required. After that the gates were removed and automatic half-barriers substituted. Control was retained by

Fig. 99 Evesham signal box and signals, looking towards Norton Junction in the down direction, March 2004.

Fig. 100 Standing on the down platform at Evesham and looking at the up signal box in the distance beyond the road bridge, March 2004.

Evesham signal box by the use of a telephone and CCTV monitoring. The farmer's crossings are user operated and connected to the box by telephone, and are the bane of a signaller's life in summer.

After 2011

The box was retained but the signals were replaced with colour lights and the single-line working towards Oxford has been replaced by AB (Fig. 101).

Moreton-in-Marsh (MM)

Date Built	1883
GWR Type or Builder	GWR Type 4B
No. of Levers	40
Ways of Working	KT, AB (AB only after 2011)
Current Status	Active
Listed (Y/N)	N

Into Gloucestershire now and it is time for a stop at a pretty Cotswold town and a crossroads. Moreton-in-Marsh was also a railway junction in that the Shipston-on-Stour branch line used to join here. Passenger services on the branch only lasted until 1929 but goods lingered on until 1960. This usually means that there will be sidings and facilities not always found at other passing stations so these places can live on after part of the original reason for their building has gone.

Fig. 101 Evesham signal box and colour light signal, August 2014.

Moreton-in-Marsh also hosted a World War II RAF bomber base, which has since become the Fire Service College.

Fig. 102 shows that the box is, windows apart, fairly original, with roof cowls and finials, steps still of wood and locking room windows together with cast iron name plate. The track behind the box was the loop line for the Shipston-on-Stour branch, which has been truncated to a siding for a track maintenance machine.

Panning back to Fig. 103, this is the Oxford Road overbridge looking back towards Evesham and Worcestershire. Note the elevated disc to signal exit from the siding, double-railed trap points and trailing crossover. The point rodding disappearing under the bridge is for the down refuge siding and

Fig. 102   Moreton-in-Marsh signal box at the end of the up platform, March 2004. To the right is Ascott-under-Wychwood and Oxford.

Fig. 103   Moreton-in-Marsh station area at the up end from the Oxford Road bridge, March 2004.

Fig. 104   Inside Moreton-in-Marsh signal box with track diagram and CCTV equipment for crossings, March 2004. Note the lowered false ceiling.

Fig. 105   Inside Moreton-in-Marsh signal box with single-line token apparatus for the Moreton-in-Marsh and Evesham section, March 2004.

trap point the other side of the bridge. Note also that the goods lockup is still in place.

Inside the box now, the track layout diagram in Fig. 104 reveals that not all the running lines are track circuited – those in black are. Parked on the block shelf are the CCTV controls and monitors for Blockley and Chipping Campden (just described as Campden) crossings.

Fig. 105 shows the single-line token apparatus at the Evesham end of the box. In boxes where there are two key token machines they tend to be at the ends of the boxes relevant to the destination to reduce the possibility of confusion with the tokens.

At the Oxford end, Fig. 106 shows some black numbered pedestal-type devices by the signal box wall, underneath the windows. These are adjusters for the signal wires in hot weather. In hot weather the signal wires expand, and if they are of appreciable length could cause the signal arm to be not fully pulled off. These adjusters take up any slack.

Finally, in the Moreton-in-Marsh box, the focus in Fig. 107 is on the absolute block equipment with Ascott-under-Wychwood. Ascott has pegged or selected Line Clear on the up line with a train running towards itself. Moreton-in-Marsh has selected Train on Line for a train coming from Ascott.

After 2011

The line to Evesham was doubled and the way of working changed to AB. The tamper machine siding and the overgrown siding on the far side have both been removed. A new low starter signal has been installed on the down side to signal a train towards Oxford from there.

Ascott-under-Wychwood (AW)

Date Built	1883
GWR Type or Builder	GWR Type 4B
No. of Levers	25
Ways of Working	AB, TCB
Current Status	Active
Listed (Y/N)	N

Progressing into Oxfordshire now, we come to Ascott-under-Wychwood, which is little more than a pretty village on the eastern edge of the Cotswolds. The station is one short platform with a 1970s-style bus shelter.

However, nearby Charlbury retains a Brunel Italianate chalet-style wooden station building, the last of its kind. The building is Grade II listed and is looked after by local people. There is also an attractive garden with seats.

Further on from Charlbury is Hanborough station, which was where the funeral train carrying Sir Winston Churchill terminated in 1965. It was returning him to his birthplace at Blenheim Palace. The train was hauled by Southern Railway Battle of Britain class Pacific, 34051 Sir Winston Churchill. There is an appeal for funds to restore this locomotive at present. The parcels van used to carry Churchill's coffin has also been retained and is currently at the National Railway Museum.

Hanborough had long been the preferred station for Blenheim Palace even though there was a closer station at Woodstock until 1954.

The box is of the same vintage as Moreton-in-Marsh but has steel steps, as can be seen in Fig. 108. The box works AB to Moreton-in-Marsh but TCB to Wolvercote Junction, north of Oxford.

Fig. 106 Still inside Moreton-in-Marsh signal box, here is the left-hand end of the lever frame with signal adjusters behind, March 2004.

Fig. 107 Moreton-in-Marsh signal box and the absolute block instruments for Ascott-under-Wychwood, March 2004.

There is also one more rearward-facing window at Ascott than Moreton to help with spotting traffic for the crossing (Fig. 109). Note the brick pillars supporting the porch end of the box and helping out the cast iron version.

It is here that the line, having been double track from Moreton-in-Marsh, reverts to single track for the run to Wolvercote Junction.

Although there are twenty-five levers in the frame, only seven remain in use. Post-2011 all that

Fig. 108   Ascott-under-Wychwood signal box, with its splendid cast iron sign, is mostly original except for the windows and door, March 2004.

Fig. 109   Ascott-under-Wychwood signal box rear view with one extra window than normal, March 2004.

has happened here is that semaphore signals have been replaced by colour light signals.

Worcester to Hereford

Fig. 110 shows another fairly short section between Worcester and Hereford. As Worcester has already been covered and Hereford is TCB with minimal mechanical signalling and will be covered elsewhere, the section covers just three signal boxes.

The line here skirts the eastern edge of the Malvern Hills, some of the most beautiful countryside in England that has been awarded Area of Outstanding Natural Beauty status. Poet W.H. Auden, who taught at a school nearby waxed lyrical about the area, as has the current poet laureate, Carol Ann Duffy, who has appeared locally at poetry readings. Sir Edward Elgar also found inspiration for his music from this area, in common with other less well-known composers and performers.

From earliest days the waters from a natural spring at Malvern have been highly regarded, and are said to have been the basis for the natural spring water industry in Britain. You can still fill up your containers here for free.

Malvern is also the home of the iconic Morgan sports car and there are hill climb events nearby to test these and other marques.

Newland East (NE)

Date Built	1900
GWR Type or Builder	GWR Type 7a
No. of Levers	33
Way of Working	AB
Current Status	Active
Listed (Y/N)	N

This signal box is about as basic as a double-line absolute block structure gets. The only slight variant is that it also controls a level crossing where the approach roads are narrow and winding, so it would not be suitable for remote CCTV control as we have seen at Chipping Campden controlled by Moreton-in-Marsh, for example. The barriers are controlled from a panel within the signal box by the signaller.

There is also a trailing crossover. The entire functionality in terms of the lever frame is ten levers from a frame of thirty-three, so most of them will be painted white.

Fig. 110 Diagrammatic representation of the signal boxes between Worcester and Hereford.

Fig. 111 Newland East signal box with the signaller at the window waiting for a train to pass so that he can raise the barriers at the control panel he is standing at, July 2014.

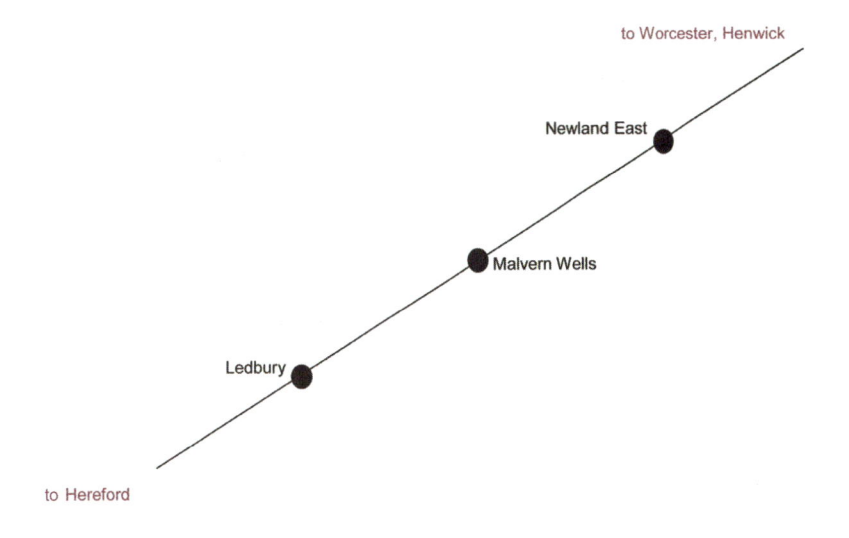

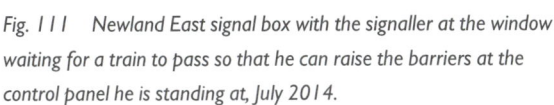

Fig. 112 Newland East roof detail, showing ventilators, roof slates and replacement flashing for ridge tiles, July 2014.

The box has many original features, including the cast name plate, although it originally was named 'Stocks Lane', roof ridge tiles and finial and cowl ventilators (Fig. 111). The signaller is at the barrier control panel and is waiting for the passage of a train to raise the barriers. The ridge tiles on the hip part of the roof appear to have been replaced with sheet lead flashing – note the ventilator fixing castings (Fig. 112). There is also a wooden staircase but it is not original.

The rear of the box is shown in Fig. 113 and what appears to be an original locking frame window enclosed in the engineer's blue brick.

Still at the rear of the box, Fig. 114 gives a view of the 'mod cons': the air-conditioning unit on a steel shelf and the back of the porch toilet block. In between these items is some older technology in the form of the coal fireplace chimney stack.

The last view at Newland East, in Fig. 115, is an earlier one of the crossover in the semi-darkness of

Fig. 113 Newland East rear detail of locking room window and side of chimney breast, July 2014.

Fig. 114 Newland East signal box rear detail of the mod cons, July 2014.

Fig. 115 Newland East signal box crossover, with signal lamps and backlights aglow, November 2005.

an evening, with the signal lamps and their backlights showing up well. The Malvern Hills beckon in the distance.

Malvern Wells (MW)

Date Built	1919
GWR Type or Builder	GWR Type 7d
No. of Levers	40
Way of Working	AB, TB
Current Status	Active
Listed (Y/N)	N

Malvern Wells signal box is between the stations of Great Malvern and the lesser, single-platform Colwall station. Great Malvern is a splendid rendition of a Victorian stone-built station, with cast iron decorated finery like the icing on a cake. It is also the terminus for some trains. Malvern Wells signal box controls the crossing-over of terminating services and their temporary storage until Great Malvern station is ready to take them. A terminating service has to be first held in the down goods loop, cross over to the up line and then be stored in the up siding in order not to disrupt through services.

The box works AB to Newland East and tokenless block (TB) to Ledbury signal box. Tokenless block is very rare now and uses special block instruments that interlock with each other at Ledbury. It locks the signals to prevent another train entering the section in the opposite direction on the single line when it is already occupied. Some of the interlocking is train operated. This system was known by the GWR as lock and block and it reduced the delays usually encountered on single lines with token exchanges.

The building is not as original as Newland East or some of the others, as there are odd ventilator cowls, uPVC windows and no cast name plate, but there are locking room windows. This box has an internal staircase and consequently no porch on which to hang the toilet block so a small cubicle outside is used. This could be extremely uncomfortable in winter (Fig. 116).

Fig. 117 shows a view of the layout from the Peachfield Road overbridge. The home signal on the right has a calling on arm for shunting moves. The elevated double disc signal on the left is for using the crossover to the up main line or for reversing into the down goods loop. The DMU looks as though it has just used the crossover and is about to reverse back down the line and into the goods loop to await its next turn of duty.

Moving to the other side of the bridge now, Fig. 118 shows a class 170 DMU train that has been signalled to go to Great Malvern station. The loop exit signal on the right is plated with a diagonally hatched plate. This is a mandatory instruction to the driver to telephone the signal box to let the signaller know when a train is safely in the goods loop. This means the signaller can reset the goods loop entry point for normal main line running. This is necessary because the signaller cannot see the entirety of the goods loop from the box or whether the whole of the train is safely in the loop.

Fig. 116   Malvern Wells signal box, August 2006.

Fig. 117 (right)   Malvern Wells signal box from the Peachfield Road overbridge, August 2006. Home signal is on the right with subsidiary arm below and double elevated discs on the left.

Fig. 118   Class 170 DMU heads for Great Malvern Station, July 2014.

Fig. 119   Lofty Ledbury signal box with replacement wooden staircase, November 2005.

Ledbury (L)

Date Built	1885
GWR Type or Builder	Mackenzie and Holland Type 3
No. of Levers	42
Way of Working	TB
Current Status	Active
Listed (Y/N)	N

Into Herefordshire and to an ancient market town that has the half-timbered buildings that are so much a hallmark of the Welsh Marches. It is also a place where the cider industry has a presence and the county has been renowned for this beverage for centuries. It is also well known for the manufacture of perry, a sparkling alcoholic beverage made from pears.

The signal box is unique as a building and its height is a function of the fact that the line curves significantly. Coming from Malvern Wells and Colwall the line burrows through the Malvern Hills for 1,316yd (1,203m) before curving out of the tunnel and into the station. The station has two platforms, separated by a loop, and from the loop on the down side, towards Hereford, is a single trailing siding.

The signal box is quite imposing for such a simple track layout but is a sign that there was an extensive goods yard with facilities for cattle, coal and general merchandise. Ledbury was also the junction for the line from Over Junction near Gloucester. This 19-mile (31km) branch line ran through Newent in the Forest of Dean, through Dymock to Ledbury. Passenger services ceased in 1959 and freight lingered on until 1962. Ledbury also had a small locomotive depot and turntable for banking or assisting trains through Ledbury tunnel.

Fig. 120 is a more detailed view of the unusual locking room windows and the attractive brickwork over them.

The view looking back towards the tunnel from the footbridge is shown in Fig. 121. The DMU on the left has arrived from Colwall and the Malverns and the home signals are telling us another train is

Fig. 120   Ledbury signal box locking frame windows with brick detail, November 2005.

Fig. 121   Ledbury looking towards Worcester, November 2005.

expected on the up line to the Malverns. Note the colour light signal angled across the track for the down line coming towards us.

Looking towards Shelwick Junction and Hereford (Fig. 122), the line resumes its single track mode once more. The branch to Over Junction and Gloucester left the down line on the left just after the steel girders of the road overbridge. The front of the DMU is almost upon the girders.

Shrewsbury Area

Shrewsbury has been a fortified town since medieval times and was the prize handed out to one of the loyal followers of William the Conqueror. It occupies a loop in the River Severn and so was seen as easy to defend from mostly Welsh invaders.

The town was never seriously industrialized except for Sentinel wagon and loco works and, more recently, Rolls Royce. It has retained much of its original character and has evolved over the years with many fine Georgian and Victorian buildings, of which Shrewsbury station is arguably the finest. When Shrewsbury station was built in 1848 in imitation Tudor style it was said to have cost £170,000, a king's ransom in today's money.

The diagram in Fig. 123 gives some idea of the interlacing of lines through and around the station but no indication of the still complex layout of it all. The signal boxes under consideration have 180, 120, 93 and 61 levers, which should convey the nature of it. Shrewsbury was a jointly owned station between the GWR and LNWR/LMS railways, so some of what follows is London and North Western Railway equipment but was used to signal trains to and from GWR destinations and in many cases using equipment of GWR parentage. In any case the LMS signed over the entirety of the working of Shrewsbury station to the GWR in 1932.

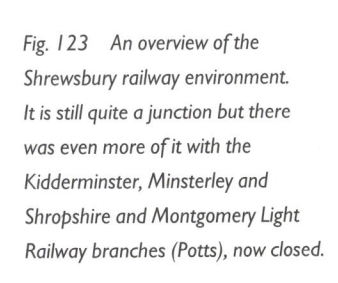

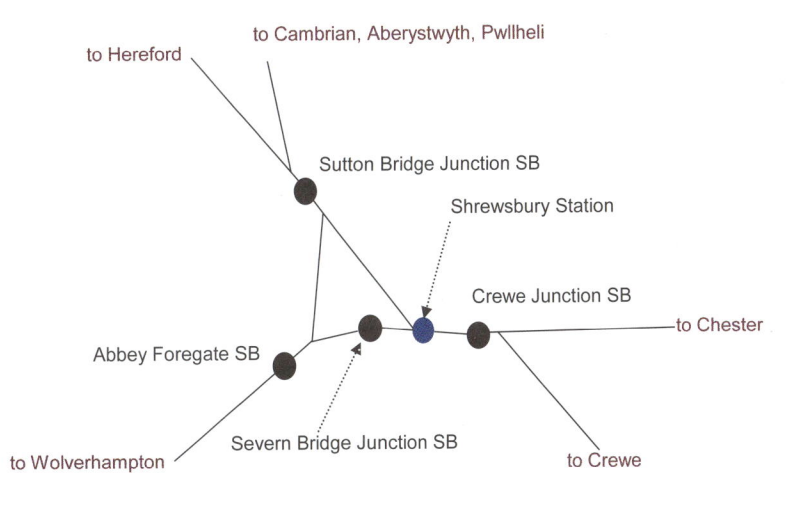

Fig. 122 Ledbury looking towards Hereford, November 2005.

Fig. 123 An overview of the Shrewsbury railway environment. It is still quite a junction but there was even more of it with the Kidderminster, Minsterley and Shropshire and Montgomery Light Railway branches (Potts), now closed.

Fig. 124 Severn Bridge Junction signal box with three different styles of signalling on show and a freight train going behind the box, July 2014.

Fig. 125 Severn Bridge Junction signal box viewed from platform 5 at Shrewsbury station, July 2014.

Severn Bridge Junction (SBJ)

Date Built	1903
GWR Type or Builder	LNWR
No. of Levers	180
Way of Working	AB
Current Status	Active
Listed (Y/N)	Y

Severn Bridge Junction signal box is monumental in every respect. With 180 levers, it is the largest (operationally) mechanical signal box in the world, although signal boxes in Britain with more than 200 levers were quite common up until the 1960s, with the last disappearing in the 1980s. Fig. 124 tries to capture some of the grandeur, and, interestingly enough, three different types of signalling can be seen: GWR/WR lower quadrant on the bracket, LMS/LMR on the single post on the left and a colour light signal with route indicator on the right. Behind the signal box is a loaded coal train from Portbury Dock near Bristol to Rugeley power station in Staffordshire. Behind that is Shrewsbury Abbey. The box looks substantially original, which it should, as Network Rail are constrained to make any updates in the style of the original as it is Grade II listed. The finials, windows, locking frame windows and timber end cladding all look as built. There are two signallers on duty during the day.

Fig. 125 is somewhat more down to earth to show the junction. The lines to the right head off to Sutton Bridge Junction and the lines to Hereford and mid-Wales on the former Cambrian lines. The latter is actually a former GWR connection to the Cambrian at Westbury (Shropshire).

The group of lines to the left go past Abbey Foregate signal box and the route to Wellington (Shropshire) and Wolverhampton. Further to the left is a fan of carriage sidings, much reduced in recent years as the tendency is for made-up sets of DMUs. The holiday excursion train made up of little-used coaching stock is largely a thing of the past.

The two groups of lines are linked by a double-track line that encloses Severn Bridge Junction in a triangle of lines. This means any train that needs to miss out Shrewsbury station on its way from Hereford to Wolverhampton or vice versa can do so. The coal train in Fig. 124 is a case in point.

Severn Bridge Junction signal box at its peak needed three signallers and a booking 'lad'. The booking lad was there solely to fill in the train register. Clearly, with several sets of block bells, the lad had to know which bell had rung and what the bell code was, note the time and then write it all down.

Fig. 126 looks back from the Abbey Foregate signal box and Wolverhampton lines. The signals in earlier years were often gantries spanning many tracks. This is a photograph from earlier years as you can see the floodlights of Shrewsbury Town's

Fig. 126   Severn Bridge Junction from the Wellington lines with class 47 approaching, January 2004.

Gay Meadow football ground between the two signal posts on the left. This pitch was so near the river that up until the 1960s a person was employed to sit in a coracle in the middle of the River Severn to retrieve a football should it be booted out of the ground and end up in the river. The ground closed in 2007.

Note the GWR corrugated iron hut in between the tracks and a class 47 with headlight, on the right heading this way. Note also in the foreground a GWR point lever complete with guard rail.

Crewe Junction (CJ)

Date Built	1903
GWR Type or Builder	LNWR
No. of Levers	120
Way of Working	AB
Current Status	Active
Listed (Y/N)	Y

Crewe Junction signal box (Fig. 127) is almost as monumental as Severn Bridge Junction and lives at the northern end of Shrewsbury station. It's another listed building and is apparently original, even boasting a timber staircase to track level. As at Severn Bridge Junction, it also has an internal staircase. It controls the station from about halfway along as well as the complex junctions with the Crewe and Chester lines.

Figure 128 shows the iceberg-like nature of Crewe Junction with a building height that is actually greater than its better-known neighbour at the other end of Shrewsbury station. Note the toilet block perched near the operating floor and the vast height of the locking frame floor, which was said to

Fig. 127 (below left)   Crewe Junction signal box, October 2003.

Fig. 128 (below right)   Crewe Junction signal box from the rear, July 2014.

Fig. 129 Crewe Junction signal box from the Chester end, showing end detail and bolt-on toilet block, July 2014.

Fig. 130 Sharp curves off the Crewe line where a Royal Mail train crashed in 1907. This picture is from September 2005.

be necessary due to the way the LNWR organized their locking frames. The uPVC fanlight door on the ground floor is an interloper though.

The Chester end of Crewe Junction signal box in Fig. 129 shows plenty of evidence of a well-maintained box, at least from the outside. On 12 October 1907 a Royal Mail train coming off the Crewe line hit the curve at an estimated 60mph (100km/h). The limit is 15mph (24km/h). The result was seventeen people killed and thirty-one badly injured. The wreckage that piled up miraculously missed the recently built Crewe Junction signal box despite the train being all across the junction.

In Fig. 130 you can see the two curves off the Crewe line, and they are both limited to 15mph. They both have a rail inside the inner running rail known as a check rail; these are only usually found on sharp curves and bridges, where derailment consequences would be more severe.

Abbey Foregate (AF)

Date Built	1914
GWR Type or Builder	GWR 7d
No. of Levers	93
Way of Working	AB, TCB
Current Status	Active
Listed (Y/N)	N

Fig. 131, showing Abbey Foregate signal box in 2004, gives us a glimpse of what original GWR signal box windows looked like. The style of glazing was known as 'three over two', where there are three small panes over two larger panes in one panel. Each panel can be slid along to open.

Compare and contrast reviews are very popular generally but Fig. 131 shows that the passage of ten years hasn't seen many changes here. The most striking is the windows. The uPVC era has probably created a more convenient and comfortable environment for the signaller but the signal box buff may deplore a box that has lost its soul through its window replacement.

Fig. 133 reflects back along the line looking past Abbey Foregate towards Wellington. There is a home and distant signal on the same post by the box and this has a theatre-type route indicator. This will have replaced a gantry, of which there were several here in the 1980s. There are also ground discs of small and larger varieties, some of which are track circuited, and a couple of GWR manual point levers that are part of the carriage siding complex that Abbey Foregate controls. A fan of sidings would be manually controlled through internal levers, but when an exit onto the main line is required, a signal box-controlled point, trap point and signal will be needed.

Fig. 131   Abbey Foregate signal box, January 2004.

Fig. 132   Abbey Foregate signal box, July 2014.

Fig. 134 is the signal referred to in the previous figure that has usurped a gantry. It appears to have a fixed distant as there is no lens in the green aspect. There is GWR-type bullhead rail in the foreground.

The final view from Abbey Foregate towards Severn Bridge Junction (Fig. 135) shows the modernized bracket array instead of the gantry technology of yesteryear.

Sutton Bridge Junction (SUB)

Date Built	1913
GWR Type or Builder	GWR 7
No. of Levers	61
Way of Working	AB, ETRMS
Current Status	Active
Listed (Y/N)	N

Fig. 133 (above)   Abbey Foregate signal box, looking back from the carriage sidings, January 2004. Note the point levers and ground discs.

Fig. 134 (left)   Abbey Foregate signal box and home and distant signal together with route indicator, January 2004.

Fig. 135 Abbey Foregate lines fanning out to the station and round to the Hereford line, July 2014.

Fig. 136 Sutton Bridge Junction signal box. The overbridge in the background has a large arch in the middle and this is where the Severn Valley line used go.

Fig. 137 Sutton Bridge Junction signal box from the rear, July 2014. Note the point rodding coming out of the back of the box, similar to Worcester Tunnel Junction.

Fig. 138 Sutton Bridge Junction signal box running lines towards Shrewsbury station and Abbey Foregate, July 2014. Note the class 37 in the track maintenance depot, the former Coleham goods yard. The Coleham engine sheds were where the light industrial building on the right is now.

Sutton Bridge Junction signal box is the smallest in the area being considered but is still busy and vital. It works AB to Dorrington on the Hereford line and ERTMS to Machynlleth on the Cambrian line through mid-Wales. It also works AB to Severn Bridge Junction.

The box is fairly original, with a splendid attempt to replicate the three over two windows of a genuine GWR box, albeit in uPVC. The ventilators have, unfortunately – according to a signaller – been targets of late-night revellers who can encircle the box in a pincer movement with footbridges on two sides, and hurl cans and bottles at them with only a modicum of success. Equally fortunately their over-indulgence has not imbued their aim with any degree of accuracy and consequently some ventilators survive. Furthermore, as a protection against these depredations, some of the windows are protected by wire netting grilles. There was graffiti on the box at some point but as only Banksy-type street art is considered suitable for GWR boxes, it has been removed.

Fig. 137 shows the rear of Sutton Bridge Junction signal box. Note the point rodding leaving the rear of the box. The enlarged rear-facing window was to enable signallers to keep an eye on trains to Kidderminster via the Severn Valley line. This would have been needed as single-line tokens would have been exchanged here. They would also have been exchanged, at one time, off the Cambrian line, but from 1987 the line was worked by RETB (radio electronic tokenless block) and from 2006 by ERTMS.

Back to the running lines, Fig. 138 looks back towards Severn Bridge Junction. You can tell this by the Abbey in the background. On the left is a recent innovation of a track maintenance depot with a resident class 37 locomotive in attendance. On this site was Coleham Goods Depot, one of seven goods yards in Shrewsbury at its peak. On the right was the joint LNW/GW locomotive sheds also known as Coleham. The bracket signal on the right had three dolls, the one on the far right for sidings and prior to that the Severn Valley Railway.

Fig. 139 looks the other way. The line straight on is to Hereford, and the Cambrian curves away towards the top of the picture. The class 175 is headed for Shrewsbury station. The line that the wagon and track workers are standing on is a headshunt from the track maintenance depot.

Still looking south, Fig. 140 shows a six-car class 158 unit coming off the Cambrian. The branch home signal is quite properly OFF. This train is an example of the increased network traffic on the network in recent years. Note the trap point on the goods loop on the left ready to derail any runaway vehicle heading for the main line.

Fig. 139 Sutton Bridge Junction signal box running lines with a class 175 coming from Hereford direction and crossing over the Cambrian junction, July 2014.

Fig. 140 Sutton Bridge Junction running lines with a class 158 coming off the Cambrian, July 2014.

Shrewsbury to Hereford

In World War I the 'Jellicoe Specials' used this as part of their route. Jellicoe Specials, named after a Royal Navy admiral, were trains that took Welsh steam coal from the South Wales valleys to the Grand Fleet at anchor at Scapa Flow off the Orkney Islands. This was a round-the-clock operation to keep the fleet fed with coal. Welsh steam coal has long been recognized as the best for boilers producing steam for propulsion.

The North to West route became invaluable during World War II as it enabled vast numbers of armed forces personnel and materiel to be moved to the south coast ports, in particular in the run-up to D-Day in June 1944. The route was towards the outer range limit for enemy bombers and did not pass through large cities, which in themselves were a target.

The diagram in Fig. 141 shows a route of some 50½ miles (81km) through Shropshire and Herefordshire. It is a journey of almost complete pleasure from a scenic point of view and not without interest for the enthusiast or modeller. It was jointly owned by the GWR and the LNWR/LMS. The route was part of that used to connect the north of England with Cardiff and the west of England via the Severn Tunnel. Typically the starting point for these trains would be Manchester,

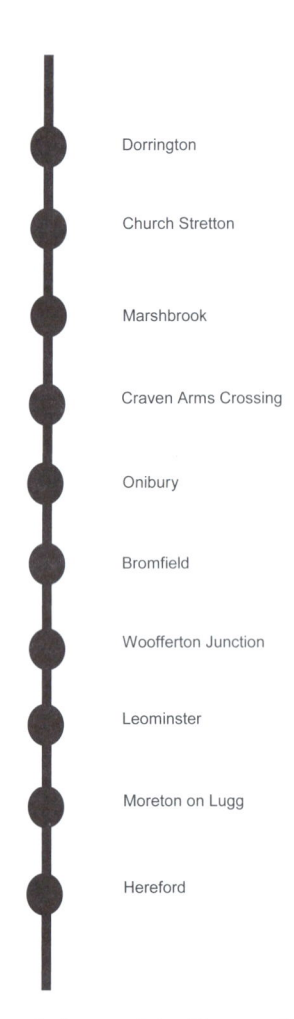

- Dorrington
- Church Stretton
- Marshbrook
- Craven Arms Crossing
- Onibury
- Bromfield
- Woofferton Junction
- Leominster
- Moreton on Lugg
- Hereford

Fig. 141 Schematic diagram of signal boxes on the Shrewsbury–Hereford line.

Fig. 142   General layout of track and inner signals at Dorrington, Shropshire, July 2014.

Liverpool or points north on the west coast main line. From the Severn Tunnel the route would go to Bristol and then all points west. This was a Monday to Saturday operation in the West Country as the Severn Tunnel was invariably shut on Sundays for maintenance.

Dorrington (DR)

Date Built	c.1872
GWR Type or Builder	LNW/GWR Jnt Type 1
No. of Levers	33
Way of Working	AB
Current Status	Active
Listed (Y/N)	N

Dorrington is about 5½ miles (9km) from Sutton Bridge Junction signal box, and appears to be in the middle of not very much. It was once a station and goods yard and home to the depot for Independent Milk Supplies. Milk would be collected and delivered to the depot and then put into glass-lined tankers and sent off on a daily trip to another IMS depot just outside Marylebone station. The trains would consist of five six-wheeled tank wagons with a total capacity of 15,000 gallons (68,100 litres), and a coach and van for support staff and equipment. Engines would be changed at Banbury in Oxfordshire as the train would then move onto the LNER for the run to Marylebone and the London depot of IMS. Clearly, milk was big at Dorrington, or at least the collection of it. This traffic ceased, the station closed and Dorrington retained the goods loops. The station site and IMS depot were sold off and are now a builder's yard.

In Fig. 142 you can see an overall view of the site with now only a crossover to control as well as the signals. The signals on the up side towards Shrewsbury, going up the page, are all London Midland Region/LMS types and the down side Western Region/GWR types – it was a joint line. The builder's yard is just in the shot, as is the added-on toilet block on the back of the box.

The general view of Dorrington in Fig. 143 is striking in that it does not resemble either GWR or LNWR signal boxes seen so far – squat, with smaller windows and a wooden board with cast iron letters applied for a name plate. There is a wooden staircase that is a fair copy of the original and uPVC windows that mimic the originals. It is also one of the oldest signal boxes still in use.

The locking frame window appears to be original and of cast iron (Fig. 144).

Taken ten years earlier, Fig. 145 shows the down goods loop still in place and GWR-type lower quadrant signals on both sides. There are two upper quadrant ground discs, however. The signal box is to the right out of shot and you can see the galvanized steel fencing of the builder's yard. The speed limit on the up line is the same.

79

Fig. 143   Dorrington signal box, July 2014.

Fig. 144   Dorrington signal box original locking frame window, July 2014.

Fig. 145   Dorrington down refuge siding, January 2004.

Church Stretton (CS)

Date Built	1872
GWR Type or Builder	LNW/GWR Jnt Type 1
No. of Levers	25
Way of Working	AB
Current Status	Demolished 2009
Listed (Y/N)	N

Church Stretton signal box was about 12 miles (19km) from Sutton Bridge Junction signal box on a continually rising gradient where Church Stretton is the summit. Although Church Stretton is the summit of the railway line the actual location with reference to the surrounding area is a depression or a 'saddle' which flooded over the years. The town has been something of a resort since the eighteenth century, especially after the railway arrived in 1852. It is the only town in Shropshire that is included in the Area of Outstanding Natural Beauty that is the Shropshire Hills. There were numerous hotels developed in Victorian times and the Long

Mynd is a prominent feature above the town that has been popular with walkers and spectators for generations.

Trains from the Central Wales line from Swansea to Shrewsbury would call here. In the 1950s these trains would be headed by ex-LMS class 5 4–6–0 or Fowler 2–6–4T locomotives.

There were serious floods in 2000 and the line was inundated. The signal box was 'switched out'. This meant that all the block instruments were bypassed such that Dorrington communicated directly with Marsh Brook, the next box south, and all Church Stretton's running signals were pulled off. By 2004 the box was not in use but still on the payroll of Network Rail (Fig. 146). The photographs date from the out-of-use era. The trailing crossover is out of use and clamped for the running lines.

Taken from the up platform of the station, which is still extant, Fig. 147 illustrates what happens when the signal box is out of use. The signal arm has been removed from the up starter. With new installations, if a signal is not in use yet, it is customary to place a white cross over the arm or the colour light lens.

The old station building, dating from 1852, is beyond the bridge on the up side. This is a private residence and is still there at the time of writing.

Thirty-seven years after steam finished in this area it was still possible to see reminders, such as the GWR water crane on the down, Hereford, side in Fig. 148. You can just see the scalloped paintwork halfway up the central post where the crane was painted in darker colours below the scalloped edge. The leather bag has long since gone but the handle that the engine crew used to grab the crane derrick with is still there. Note the de-armed signal on its post but ground disc still with its disc.

Fig. 146   Church Stretton signal box – still on the books but on the way out, January 2004.

Fig. 147 (right centre)   Church Stretton up starter signal minus arm, January 2004.

Fig. 148 (right)   Church Stretton armless signal and steam-age water crane, January 2004.

Fig. 149   Marshbrook signal box, Shropshire, January 2004.

Fig. 150   Marshbrook signal box side view, the Hereford end, January 2004.

Marshbrook (MB)

Date Built	1872
GWR Type or Builder	LNW/GWR Jnt Type 1
No. of Levers	18
Way of Working	AB
Current Status	Active
Listed (Y/N)	Y

The village of Marshbrook (or sometimes Marsh Brook) is just off the A49, and the signal box is easily visible from the road. It is at the junction with the B4370 towards Bishop's Castle, another delightful small town in south Shropshire that had its own railway once. Marshbrook had its own station and goods facilities across the crossing.

Fig. 149 shows a remarkably original box that has a certified construction date of 1872 and is one of the oldest on NR. It was thought so important to the history of signal boxes that, on the news that all signal boxes were to be got rid of, English Heritage listing and Grade II status were awarded in 2013.

Fig. 151   Marshbrook signal box rear view, looking a bit rebuilt, January 2004.

Fig. 152   Marshbrook signal box side view, the Shrewsbury end, January 2004.

The figures 15.29 on the front of the box relate to the fact that this box is 15 miles and 29 chains (24.7km) from English Bridge Junction at Shrewsbury, which is where the lines for the station and avoiding lines round the back of Severn Bridge Junction signal box split.

Fig. 150 is a side view of the Hereford end of the box with the village across the crossing to the left. Since Church Stretton's removal, the box works AB to Dorrington in the north and Craven Arms in the south towards Hereford.

Figs 151 and 152 are the rear and Shrewsbury side end of the box. The sign for the garage on the A49 can be seen in Fig. 152 and the stationmaster's house, although extended, is on the right.

Fig. 153 Craven Arms Crossing signal box, the Shrewsbury end, January 2004.

Craven Arms Crossing (CA)

Date Built	1947
GWR Type or Builder	GWR Type 34
No. of Levers	30
Way of Working	AB, NSTR
Current Status	Active
Listed (Y/N)	N

Craven Arms is a pleasant market town and road junction that has a historic castle nearby at Stokesay – in fact, Craven Arms station used to be known as Craven Arms and Stokesay.

Craven Arms was a junction of some importance and had a station, three signal boxes, engine and carriage sheds and a goods depot to support the activities there. It still is a junction for the ex-LNWR Central Wales line and has single-line working for that as well as AB for the boxes at Marshbrook and Onibury either side on the Shrewsbury–Hereford line. In the past Craven Arms was also the junction for the lines to Bishop's Castle and Much Wenlock. The actual point work of the last two junctions was a little way away from Craven Arms but all the traffic had to be exchanged there.

At first sight the box in Fig. 153 is reminiscent of a small industrial shed of 1990s vintage and is most unattractive. The outer shell, however, masks a genuine GWR signal box that had structural problems. The lower half of the building is substantially original but clad with the industrial corrugated sheet, while the box top was taken away piecemeal and replaced with the garden shed style as seen. In recent years Network Rail have introduced some sensitivity into signal box architecture and even copy styles of a bygone age – Stallingborough in north Lincolnshire comes to mind as an example.

Fig. 154 looks south towards Hereford. The Central Wales line branches to the right and there is a notice trackside to warn the driver about the token. This section is NSTR, which is no signaller token remote. The driver is issued with the token at both ends but has to swap tokens along the route and operate the token instruments without a signaller present. The tracks to Hereford drop away sharply and the signals over the brow are not visible from the signal box.

Fig. 155 was taken from the footbridge at Craven Arms station looking up towards Shrewsbury. The box is on the right of the running lines just before the lines curve away. The building on the same side but nearer is the former goods shed. There are trailing and facing crossovers here, which is unusual but the facing one is needed so that down trains can get over to the Central Wales line as required. There is also a goods loop on the down side and a

Fig. 154   The view from Craven Arms station footbridge looking towards Hereford, August 2014.

Fig. 155   The view from Craven Arms station footbridge looking towards Shrewsbury, August 2014.

permanent way siding on the up. The speed limits on the up are 90mph (145km/h) for DMUs and 40mph (64km/h) for everything else.

The next two figures feature a couple of trains to give the flavour of operations at Craven Arms. Fig. 156 is a return empty working of the coal train we saw passing behind the back of Severn Bridge Junction signal box in Fig. 124. This train is running back to Stoke Gifford sidings near Bristol to await the next load of coal and possibly the next ship at Portbury Dock.

Class 175 of Chester depot hurries northwards towards Shrewsbury in Fig. 157. Note the two home signals OFF for the train. The signaller will not give train out of section until the rear of the train and tail lamp has been observed passing the box. The left-hand, taller arm of the bracket signal is for the down Hereford direction and the shorter right hand for the facing crossover to access the Central Wales line. Note the permanent way siding by the DMU. The two point rods going up the left-hand side are one for the crossover and one for the facing point locks.

Fig. 158 shows the inside of Craven Arms box and the control panel for the lifting barriers and flashing red lights. It was possible for a signaller to lift a barrier while a train was on the crossing. This cannot now happen (*see* the section on Moreton on Lugg late in this chapter for more details).

A fine display of levers is shown in the frame at Craven Arms in Fig. 159. The blue/brown lever reversed at the end of the frame is for the crossing wicket gates. The two levers with black and white chevrons are to place detonators on the track as a

Fig. 156   A class 66 and coal train empties heading for Stoke Gifford sidings, August 2014.

Fig. 157 A class 175 Coradia heading towards Shrewsbury, August 2014.

warning to engine crews during fog. Detonators placed by lever are not used any longer but the levers remain. The lever collars placed over two of the signal handles are a Network Rail innovation. Lever collars are reminders to signallers not to operate particular levers, usually if a train is standing in section, although the block instruments have similar reminders.

Between the levers and the front wall of the box are black, tripod-like objects with a winding handle on top. These winders are used to adjust the signal wires of the signals further away from the box when a rise in outside air temperature causes the signal wires to expand.

Another fine display on the block shelf appears in Fig. 160. The GWR 1947 instruments are showing a Train on Line to Marshbrook and Line Clear given for a train coming from Onibury in the Hereford direction. The block bells sound quite different in their tone.

Finally, in Craven Arms signal box there is the single-line token apparatus for the Central Wales line. Above the instrument and placed on the block

Fig. 158 Craven Arms Crossing signal box, the lifting barriers control panel, August 2014.

Fig. 159 Craven Arms Crossing signal box, the lever frame, August 2014.

Fig. 160   Craven Arms Crossing signal box, the block shelf and instruments, August 2014.

Fig. 161   Craven Arms Crossing signal box, the single line token apparatus, August 2014.

Fig. 162   Rewinding ten years at Craven Arms to show the six steam-age road carriage sheds, January 2004.

shelf is a locked box, to which the signaller has the key, to provide written authority to proceed in the event of a failure of the token apparatus.

As an epilogue on Craven Arms, the view in Fig. 162 is from ten years earlier and shows the six road carriage sheds from steam days. It is now a housing estate.

Onibury (OY)

Date Built	1977
GWR Type or Builder	BR (WR) Type 37
No. of Levers	Nil
Way of Working	AB
Current Status	Active
Listed (Y/N)	N

Onibury lies on the A49 between Craven Arms and Ludlow and astride the line with a crossing. The attractive station is still there although in use privately now. It is a pleasant village in rolling countryside with a historic church, St Michael's, some of which dates from Norman times.

The signal box has no levers in that the controls are operated by individual function switches (IFS) in a panel. There are no semaphore signals here then. This is another product of the garden shed style of architecture and it is remarkable that so little care was taken to fit it into its environment. Onibury has survived where other signal boxes like

Fig. 163   Onibury signal box between Craven Arms and Bromfield, Ludlow, April 2007.

Fig. 164   Onibury station building, April 2007.

Church Stretton have not by virtue of the crossing gates being signaller operated. Onibury is 22 miles and 68 chains (36.8km) from Shrewsbury and about halfway between Ludlow and Craven Arms.

Fig. 164 is of Onibury station building, almost exactly opposite the signal box.

Bromfield (BD)

Date Built	1873
GWR Type or Builder	LNW/GWR Jnt Type 1
No. of Levers	29
Way of Working	AB
Current Status	Active
Listed (Y/N)	N

Bromfield is near Ludlow, and while Ludlow was a junction and had its own signal box, Bromfield was retained in favour of Ludlow as it also has a crossing. Ludlow is an exceptionally pretty town on the River Teme with a castle and outdoor markets. It is a gourmet's bolthole with more Michelin-recommended restaurants per head of population than anywhere else in Britain.

Bromfield's claim to fame is its closeness to Ludlow racecourse. Unfortunately this proximity did not prevent the station and goods yard closing.

Fig. 165 shows that Bromfield signal box might be termed a bit of a mongrel in that only half of the windows have been modified – the two ends. In addition it retains its chimney stack and chimney pot despite having the modernized form of heating. Locking room windows and frames appear original.

Note the abandoned platform waiting shelter on the same down side as the box. The station building proper is on the up side, but the main platforms were on the other side of the crossing where there was enough room to build the long platforms needed for excursion trains from Birmingham.

Fig. 165   Bromfield signal box, minus name plate, near Ludlow, August 2014.

Fig. 166 Bromfield signal box, from Shrewsbury end, March 2005.

Fig. 167 Bromfield bracket signal detail, August 2014.

Fig. 168 Bromfield crossing train detector to prevent inadvertent raising of the barriers, August 2014.

There were horse unloading docks on both sides and the down side one is still there.

Fig. 166, the Bromfield signal box from the rear, shows the original chimney stack with later addition and pot. There are usually two reasons why a stack has been modified: the original one fell or was blown down; or there was insufficient draught on the coal fire with shorter stack.

Fig. 167 shows a detail of Bromfield signal box's down home bracket signal. The left-hand side of the bellcrank is pulled down when the signal lever is pulled or reversed. This means the wire at the top moves to the left and another bellcrank further on transmits this movement to pull the signal arm off. The extra holes in the bellcrank are to increase or decrease the movement for a pull. If the down wire is moved along towards the centre pivot, the pull distance is reduced – in other words the wire is effectively tightened. On the other hand, if the top wire is moved to the next hole left along towards the centre pivot the movement is increased, or the wire seems slacker. There are separate devices in signal boxes to tighten signal wire in hot weather.

Fig. 168 shows a detail of Bromfield signal box crossing. Following an incident at Moreton on Lugg (*see* later in this chapter), sensors have been installed at signaller-controlled crossings that inhibit the raising of barriers until a train has safely passed over the crossing.

Woofferton Junction (W)

Date Built	*c.*1875
GWR Type or Builder	LNW/GWR Jnt Type 1+
No. of Levers	39
Way of Working	AB
Current Status	Active
Listed (Y/N)	N

Continuing our journey south to the other side of Ludlow, we come to Woofferton Junction, which is a junction no more, like so many others, but retains the name. The junction part of the title refers to the Tenbury Wells and Bewdley branch.

Fig. 169 Woofferton Junction signal box near Ludlow, looking towards Shrewsbury, November 2004.

Fig. 170 Woofferton Junction signal box, Hereford end view, August 2014.

There was a connecting line between what is now the Severn Valley Railway at Bewdley and Woofferton Junction. A significant town considered a resort in Victorian times, Tenbury Wells was part way along the route. The branch closed from Woofferton in 1961 and the Bewdley to Tenbury Wells section continued for about another year. Woofferton station had three platforms, goods shed and a good number of sidings. The goods shed and station building survive and once again they survive as part of a builder's yard. Woofferton even had a small engine shed but that closed many years previously although the building lasted into the 1960s.

Looking at Fig. 169 and bearing the + symbol in the builder part of the table in mind, we can see that this is a much larger box than any of the joint boxes looked at so far. The frame has thirty-nine levers and that has been reduced from a total of seventy-five at its peak when the branch was open. The bracket signal is for the goods loop, which we have already seen earlier on in the book, and the junction for Tenbury Wells and Bewdley was about where the down home on the left side of the track is in the distance. The remains of the overbridge by the bracket signal are either from a farmer's occupation crossing or minor road.

Fig. 170 offers an end view of Woofferton Junction, with the air conditioning pack seemingly precariously perched outside the box. It has modernized windows and staircase.

Fig. 171 is a rear and side view of Woofferton Junction box and the truncated chimney stack and uPVC windows all round. The end nearest the reader appears to have been rebuilt as some stage.

Most definitely unmodernized is the next structure, right by Woofferton Junction box (Fig. 172). This is a GWR lamp hut in the well-known corrugated iron school of architecture that was used for many subsidiary structures. The lamp hut was where the signal lamps would be refilled, wick trimmed and lamp glasses cleaned. This would originally have been daily, then weekly, until lamps were replaced by electrical lights. The hut was painted in black gas tar, which probably explains why it has lasted so long. Other huts were painted in the company's colours.

Woofferton Junction general layout is shown in Fig. 173. The former goods shed is on the right

Fig. 171 Woofferton Junction signal box, Shrewsbury end and side view, August 2014.

Fig. 172 Woofferton Junction signal box GWR lamp hut, August 2014.

Fig. 173 Woofferton Junction signal box track and inner signal layout, August 2014.

and in front of that, hidden by trees, is the former station building. The crossovers permit either up or down trains to access the goods loop, which is on the up side. Woofferton Junction is 32 miles and 2 chains (51.5km) from English Bridge Junction at Shrewsbury and is the most southerly point in Shropshire on the railway.

Leominster (LE)

Date Built	c.1875
GWR Type or Builder	LNW/GWR Jnt Type 1+
No. of Levers	30
Way of Working	AB
Current Status	Active
Listed (Y/N)	N

Leominster is the first stop in Herefordshire and was a considerable junction in past years. It had three signal boxes, station, goods yard and a two road engine shed. The branches were to Bromyard and Worcester to the east and Presteign and New Radnor to the west.

Leominster itself is a delightful Welsh Marches town that is well known for its half-timbered buildings and a considerable trade in antiques. Leominster is 38 miles and 60 chains (62.4km) from Shrewsbury.

Fig. 174 dates from 2004; the box had been modernized even then but retained a patched-up wooden staircase, and the wall next to the staircase has a cast iron strengthener inserted.

Fast forward ten years to Fig. 175 and the box is much the same, but the staircase has gone to a galvanized steel one with a substantial steel fence around that end of the box.

Another contemporary view, Fig. 176 is of the rear of the box. The box now has a bricked-up chimney breast.

Fig. 177 gives the wider picture, looking back up the line to Shrewsbury and most of the track layout at Leominster. Facing and trailing crossovers enable trains to access the ballast/refuge siding. The station is a short way in the opposite direction.

Fig. 174   Leominster signal box, November 2004.

Fig. 175   Leominster signal box end view, August 2014.

Moreton on Lugg (ML)

Date Built   1943
GWR Type or Builder   GWR Type 12a
No. of Levers   44
Way of Working   AB, TCB
Current Status   Active
Listed (Y/N)   N

Moreton on Lugg is 46 miles and 65 chains (75.3km) from English Bridge Junction, Shrewsbury and became a minor junction, though never called that, late in the day.

During World War II the army established a network of munitions dumps here, with a junction off the up line. In later years the depot was a general stores area.

Later still, with the SAS based at nearby Hereford, the depot was used to store BR Mark 1 coaches for the SAS to attack in simulated training for a train hijack scenario in the UK. The coaches were notable in having broken windows caused, it is thought, by the use of stun grenades.

The depot is now an industrial estate.

Moreton on Lugg has a claim to infamy in that in 2010 a signaller raised the barrier whilst a train was approaching and a woman car driver was killed as a result. Another vehicle was struck on the opposite carriageway, injuring two people. There already existed a device that could be used to sense the approach of a train and lock the barriers until after

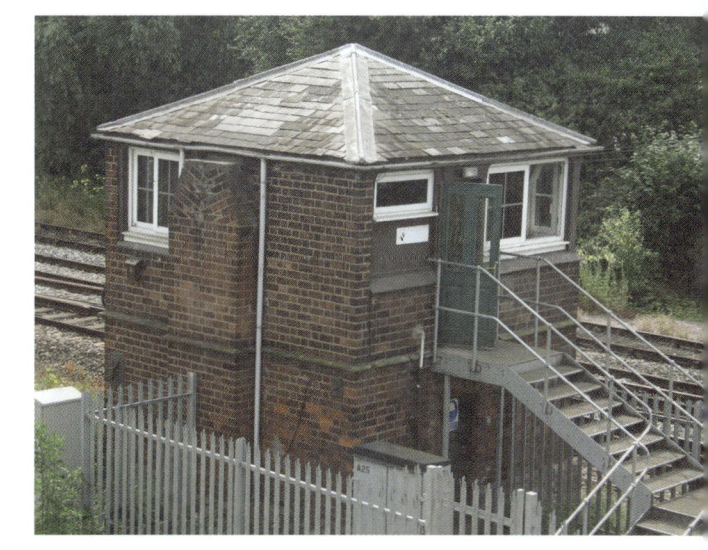

Fig. 176   Leominster signal box side and end view, August 2014.

Fig. 177   Leominster signal box track layout, August 2014.

Fig. 178   Moreton on Lugg signal box, April 2005.

Fig. 179   Moreton on Lugg signal box, Hereford end and side view, April 2005.

Fig. 180   Moreton on Lugg signal box rodding and signal wires, August 2014.

Fig. 181   Moreton on Lugg crossover and depot entry siding, August 2014.

the train had crossed, but it had not been fitted at Moreton on Lugg in 2010. It is now.

Fig. 178 shows a departure from the normal joint line box with a GWR type. The corrugated roof is a possible war-time economy measure. Cast name plate and cowl ventilators as well as locking frame windows give an original feel despite the main windows. Moreton on Lugg works AB to Leominster and TCB to Hereford.

The rear of Moreton on Lugg reveals no air-conditioning or evidence of a fireplace, as the GWR had gone to pot-bellied stoves by this time (Fig. 179). The heritage telegraph pole with pot insulators is a rarity these days – perhaps it is carrying fibre-optic cabling.

Fig. 180 shows the output of signal wires and point rodding coming out of the front of the box. Point rodding way back in time was round and now is rectangular – note the transition on the angle cranks.

Fig. 181 is where some of it goes to. There is the trailing crossover, junction for the depot and signalling looking towards Shrewsbury. Note the down outer home on the curve in the distance.

A glance now through the locking frame window at Moreton on Lugg (Fig. 182) for a glimpse of how some of the interlocking works.

Fig. 182 Moreton on Lugg signal box, part of the locking frame, August 2014.

Hereford (H)

Date Built	1884
GWR Type or Builder	LNW/GWR Jnt Type 2
No. of Levers	60
Way of Working	AB, TCB, TB
Current Status	Active
Listed (Y/N)	N

Hereford is another ancient and attractive city on the Welsh Marches with a celebrated cathedral. The cathedral contains a unique medieval artefact – the Mappa Mundi, in Latin, or Map of the World. It is a unique idea of a medieval scholar's view of the world and is believed to date from 1300. It is said to have been made using the skin of a calf, as paper products were way in the future.

Hereford has also been the headquarters of the cider-making industry, with the fruits from the orchards of Herefordshire ending up mostly as liquid whereas neighbouring Worcestershire generally moved the fruit out of the county in one piece.

Hereford cattle are renowned for the quality of their beef and their docility.

Hereford was also the meeting point, not only of the joint GWR/LNWR line from Shrewsbury, but also of the Midland Railway. It could be said Hereford had everything railway at least twice.

The GWR/LNWR station at Barr's Court is an architectural gem as befits the county town of Herefordshire, although from a mechanical signalling point of view it is of less interest as it is mostly TCB and colour light signals. Hereford works AB to

Consider the flat bar on the far left that is painted a silvery colour and the steel pegs located on a sliding board just behind the flat bar. At the top of the flat bar is a cut-out section that will engage with one of the pegs next to it if the conditions are right. The flat bar and peg seem to be touching in the photograph. The other flat bars have sections cut out but are not the same as the one on the left.

It is the cut-outs in the flat bars and the pegs' relative movement to each other that form the basis of mechanical interlocking. There are different types of this but the principles are the same. In a box with many levers the setting up of the mechanical interlocking is a major task. There can also be electrical solenoids on a mechanical frame where mechanical interlocking is not possible or practicable.

The last image from Moreton on Lugg (Fig. 183) shows the bracket for the depot siding and up main line.

Fig. 183 Moreton on Lugg signal box bracket signal, April 2005.

Fig. 184   Hereford signal box, April 2005.

Fig. 185   Hereford station and signal box general view, April 2005.

Tram Inn in the south, TB to Ledbury in the east and AB to Moreton on Lugg in the north.

Fig. 184 shows a squat building built like that so signallers could see under the canopy of the nearby Barr's Court station. The roof is more of a chalet style with an overhang and is quite unlike its other joint cousins further up the line. The chimney stack and chimney have survived, and although this view is from 2005, more recent photographs suggest it is still the same. The lines running past the box to the right form the lines to Newport. At the other end of the station are the tracks to Shrewsbury. Just over 3 miles (5km) from the box is Shelwick Junction, where the single track from Ledbury and Worcester, covered previously in the book, runs in.

Fig. 185 is a general view of Hereford station and gives the signal box's relationship to it. There are just two wire-worked ground disc signals on view. This is towards Newport.

Some of the fine detail at Hereford station, and particularly the carved stone window surrounds, appear in Fig. 186. Note also the clock from Joyce of Whitchurch. Joyce supplied many station clocks, as did Gents of Leicester.

Also of note is the GWR early – pre-1934 – station seat, albeit with replacement timbers.

Fig. 186   Hereford station detail and Joyce clock, April 2005.

Fig. 187   A class 60 and steel products empties for Llanwern, April 2005.

Fig. 188   Hereford signal box from Shrewsbury end, April 2005.

Cast ironwork on the canopy is a standard Victorian railway station feature but the theme in the castings varies usually depicting a crest or coat of arms.

Resuming the theme of traffic on the Shrewsbury Hereford line, in Fig. 187 a class 60 brings a train of steel products empties from Dee Marsh Junction near Shotton steelworks in North Wales to Llanwern in South Wales. This has been a regular working since steelmaking finished at Shotton in the 1980s. The platform roads are loops so the train is possibly being held there whilst a faster service overtakes it.

Our final view of Hereford signal box with its wooden staircase and some GWR 'spear' fencing on the A465 road overbridge behind is Fig. 188. Note the AWS ramp in the foreground. Hereford signal box is 51 miles and 13 chains (82.3km) from Shrewsbury.

Hereford to Newport, South Wales

From the rolling lush countryside of Herefordshire to equally attractive and even hillier Monmouthshire our journey continues on to join the GWR South Wales main line at Newport. The route's gradients become more demanding and this was the scene of epic struggles of steam versus gravity. There were many occasions where banking or assist engines were needed.

The line was not jointly owned from Hereford so the signal boxes from here on were built by either GWR or a contractor to the GWR.

The diagram in Fig. 189 shows the route south from Hereford to Newport in South Wales in terms of the remaining mechanical signalling. The line through to Newport station does not include Park Junction, which we have already seen; it is on the Ebbw Vale line so is not included.

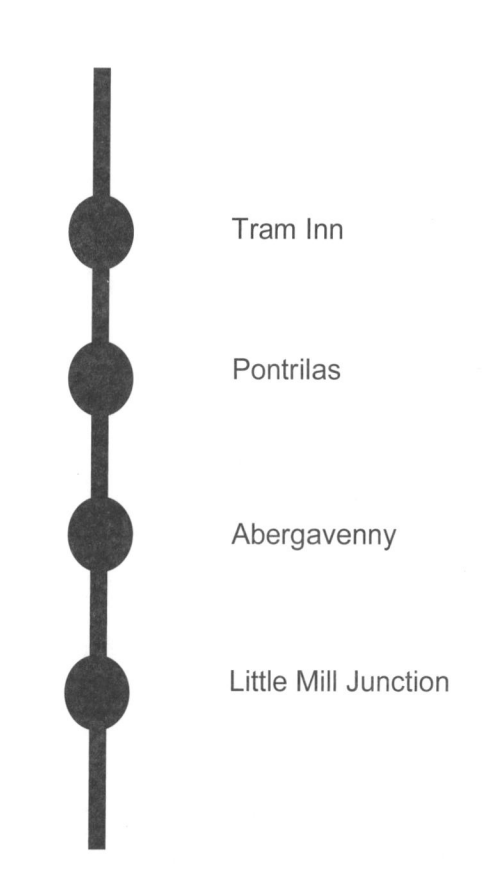

Fig. 189   Schematic diagram of Hereford–Newport signal boxes.

Fig. 190   Tram Inn signal box, April 2006.

Fig. 191   Tram Inn signal box, Newport end view, April 2006.

Tram Inn (TI)

Date Built	1894
GWR Type or Builder	GWR Type 5
No. of Levers	23
Way of Working	AB
Current Status	Active
Listed (Y/N)	N

Tram Inn is 5 miles and 37 chains (8.8km) from a point just after the Eign river bridge near Hereford. It is one of the few signal boxes named after a pub. The pub is opposite the box across the running lines (Fig. 190).

The locking frame windows are a curious mix of the usual and the round-topped variety, while the roof appears to have the 'plastic slate' replacements instead of the original Dinorwic or Penrhyn quarry originals. There is an early example of the health and safety-type steel staircase.

Fig. 191 affords a glimpse of the pub that the signal box is named after. Like so many other public houses, it has another use: at the survey date it was a garage. The bargeboards are peeling paint, and with the cladding and the main windows replaced with uPVC it seems odd that they weren't plasticized at the same time. The chimney stack on this one only starts at the first floor, which is unusual.

Fig. 192   Tram Inn signal box trailing crossover and ground discs, April 2006.

Coal was often delivered to a signal box straight from the bunker or tender of a locomotive. Platelayers or other track workers would bring a lump of coal to the box in exchange for a cup of tea. Lumps of coal would quite often fall from the tender of a fast-moving locomotive and track workers were sometimes struck, occasionally with fatal consequences.

In Fig. 192 you can see how the line curves towards Hereford and the need for the bracket on the home signal. Also you can see the ground disc, which would be OFF when a train was backing into the goods loop on the down side.

Pontrilas (PS)

Date Built	1880
GWR Type or Builder	Mackenzie and Holland Type 3 (GWR)
No. of Levers	42
Way of Working	AB
Current Status	Active
Listed (Y/N)	N

Pontrilas is only half a mile from the Welsh border, and the name means bridge over three rivers. Its name suggests it may have changed hands in earlier days.

Pontrilas had its own station and the main building survives as a guest house. Goods facilities were extensive and the area has long been known for forestry and the harvesting of timber. Pontrilas Sawmills survives to this day, although all traffic now goes by road. It retains a goods loop on the up side towards Hereford together with a headshunt siding off the goods loop. There is also a trailing crossover to enable down trains to reverse into the loop if required.

In days past there was a branch line to Hay-on-Wye but before this venue caught on as a haven for bibliophiles, the branch shut down. There was a single road engine shed off the branch to service it. The branch left the main line almost immediately after where the signal box is now, in line with the up goods loop.

The signal box was refurbished in 2009 and every effort seemingly has been taken to retain its original character. That a timber signal box should survive for over 130 years is remarkable enough, but the box must look as good now as it ever did. The wooden staircase is a replacement and there is no cast name plate. The windows are a sympathetic replacement and the finials and ventilator cowls like new. The photoelectric cell array to the right of the box is a modern addition but could hardly replace the battery cabinets of old as it does not deliver much power.

Approaching from Newport in Fig. 194 is a class 175 Coradia unit, and as Pontrilas is on a succession of curves, bracket signals abound. The subsidiary

Fig. 193   Pontrilas signal box, October 2011.

Fig. 194   Class 175 Coradia heads past Pontrilas signal box for Hereford, October 2011.

Fig. 195   Rear of Pontrilas signal box before refurbishment, April 2006.

Fig. 196   General layout at Pontrilas, April 2006.

doll is for the up goods loop, the headshunt of which is in the right foreground. There is bullhead rail in the siding and the buffer stops are also constructed from it. Flat-bottomed rail started to replace bullhead rail on running lines in a major way in the 1950s.

Fig. 195 shows Pontrilas signal box from the rear with a girder to support the rear of the box over a void. The porch, which is a recent addition, seems much more rickety than its far older host.

The Pontrilas general layout with up goods loop, headshunt and inner home bracket signals, is shown in Fig. 196. The rail built buffer stop has lost one of its planks, which would not seem to be a problem given the rustiness of the headshunt rails. As you can see, the speed limit in the up direction is 80mph (129km/h) and in the down 70mph (113km/h).

Fig. 197 shows Pontrilas tunnel and station building, now a guest house, looking towards Newport. The home signal is for the down side on the left-hand side of the left-hand track, but a better view by train crews can be had from here. It also has a sighting board as the background can act as a camouflage at this location. Pontrilas signal box is 11 miles and 21 chains (18.1km) from Hereford.

Fig. 197   Looking towards Newport at Pontrilas, October 2011. The station building is now a guest house.

Fig. 198 Abergavenny signal box, April 2006.

Abergavenny (AY)

Date Built	1934
GWR Type or Builder	GWR Type 28B
No. of Levers	52
Way of Working	AB
Current Status	Active
Listed (Y/N)	N

Abergavenny in Monmouthshire is the first signal box encountered over the Welsh border and the town itself is a delightful market town that retains a character all its own. There has been a settlement here since Roman times and it is a centre for agriculture, with a lively cattle market.

The market hall is also used for antiques fairs, farmers' markets and food fairs. The countryside around is mountainous with the Holy Mountain and Sugar Loaf mountains prominent. The trains from Craven Arms to Swansea (LNWR) on the Central Wales line battle with Sugar Loaf mountain.

There was a junction north of Abergavenny with the LNWR line to Merthyr Tydfil, and while that was open the current station was known as Abergavenny (Monmouth Road).

The station at Abergavenny is remarkably original and except for signage and other details hasn't changed much since the 1950s in steam days. The summit of the line is at Llanvihangel (known colloquially as 'Land of the Angels') Summit, 3½ miles (5.5km) towards Hereford. Many of the trains would have needed banking assistance, and Abergavenny did have an engine shed in past years.

The signal box is another all-timber box in very good condition, but this time with an internal staircase (Fig. 198). As with larger locations this box was not alone, and to distinguish it from others it was known as Abergavenny Junction. Abergavenny works AB to Pontrilas and TCB to Little Mill Junction.

Abergavenny signal box and track layout with immediate signalling are shown in Fig. 199. On the up side on the right there is a goods loop with

Fig. 199 General layout at Abergavenny, April 2006.

Fig. 200 Abergavenny station, April 2006.

headshunt and a further loop off the goods loop; perhaps this was to enable a locomotive to run round a train without encroaching onto the main line. There is also a further loop beyond these two loops; the starter signal for this is in the distance on the right-hand side some way from the main running lines.

On the down side on the right there is a refuge siding with short headshunt. The bracket signal carries the outer home and starter to come out of the refuge siding.

A glimpse now of Abergavenny station in Fig. 200, which retains a splendid buffet as well as waiting room and toilets. The up platform on the left must be twice as long as the down. The home

Fig. 201 Abergavenny up inner home with calling on arm, April 2006.

Fig. 202 Abergavenny station down platform with starter, April 2006.

Fig. 203 Abergavenny station up platform with departing class 158, April 2006.

signals for the up platform retain a calling on arm so it is possible to have two trains at the platform. The grassy expanse behind the down platform used to be occupied by a bay platform for the LNWR Merthyr trains when that branch was open and there was also a goods avoiding line running parallel with the bay platform.

The inner home with calling on arm to allow trains into the platform when already occupied, referred to above, is shown in Fig. 201.

At the opposite end of Abergavenny station the down starter signal proves that the brackets are tailor-made to suit the location (Fig. 202). Note the footbridge in the background that used to span the two other tracks as mentioned under Fig. 200.

In Fig. 203 class 158 departs along the improbably long up platform for Hereford past a lowered platform starter. Note the GWR platform seats with planks instead of discrete timbers, and all the facilities available at this station.

Abergavenny is 22 miles and 76 chains (36.9km) from Hereford.

Little Mill Junction (LM)

Date Built	c.1883
GWR Type or Builder	Mackenzie & Holland Type 3 (GWR)
No. of Levers	17
Way of Working	AB, TCB
Current Status	Active
Listed (Y/N)	N

Little Mill Junction in Monmouthshire is a fringe box to the Newport Power signal box and as such works TCB to it and AB to Abergavenny. Like Woofferton Junction, it is no longer a junction in the accepted sense.

It was previously the junction for the line running in from Monmouth and had a passenger station and goods facilities. In the era of the Jellicoe Specials in World War I (*see* the introduction to the Shrewsbury to Hereford section), Little Mill Junction developed into a storage yard for the returning trains of empty wagons from Scotland. The massive yards at Pontypool Road, a few miles to the south, were unable to cope and in any case that site had been developed almost as much as space would allow.

After the passenger line to Monmouth closed the line was kept open to transport workers (13,000 at its peak) to the Royal Ordnance Factory at Glascoed. ROF Glascoed's claim to fame is that they produced the Barnes Wallis bouncing bomb that was used by RAF 617 Squadron over the Ruhr area of Germany during World War II. When the ROF closed the branch became a siding.

Little Mill Junction signal box in Fig. 204 is similar to Pontrilas but has a brick ground floor. It has retained its wooden staircase and finials but has an attached later porch. The locking frame windows are bricked up; although in a rural location, perhaps it was thought to be vulnerable to attack in World War II, being close to a munitions factory.

Little Mill Junction signal box interior and layout diagram is shown in Fig. 205. The only mechanical signals are those to do with the branch siding. Note the black track-circuited sections and the blue ones without track circuit. Unusually it has a facing crossover.

Fig. 206 shows Little Mill Junction signal box 'NX', or entry and exit, panel, with Little Mill

Fig. 204 Little Mill Junction signal box, April 2006.

Fig. 205 Little Mill Junction signal box diagram, April 2006.

Junction towards the far end and Panteg and Griffithstown loops – to do with a steelworks and a glassmaker – almost in the centre of the picture.

Little Mill Junction signal box interior is shown in Fig. 207, and on the NEC Multisync monitor in the foreground is the Trust computer display, which gives a live visual commentary on where the trains are and if they've been subject to any delay. The desk and register remain though.

Little Mill Junction signal box is seen together with mechanical signalling in Fig. 208. The rest of the installation is colour light signals.

Fig. 206 Little Mill Junction signal box NX panel, April 2006.

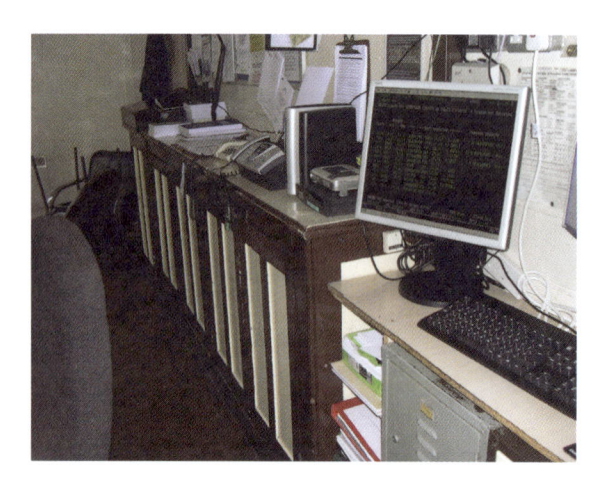

Fig. 207 Little Mill Junction signal box, Trust screen, desk and register, April 2006.

Fig. 208 Little Mill Junction signal box and mechanical signalling, April 2006.

Fig. 209 North Warwickshire line schematic diagram.

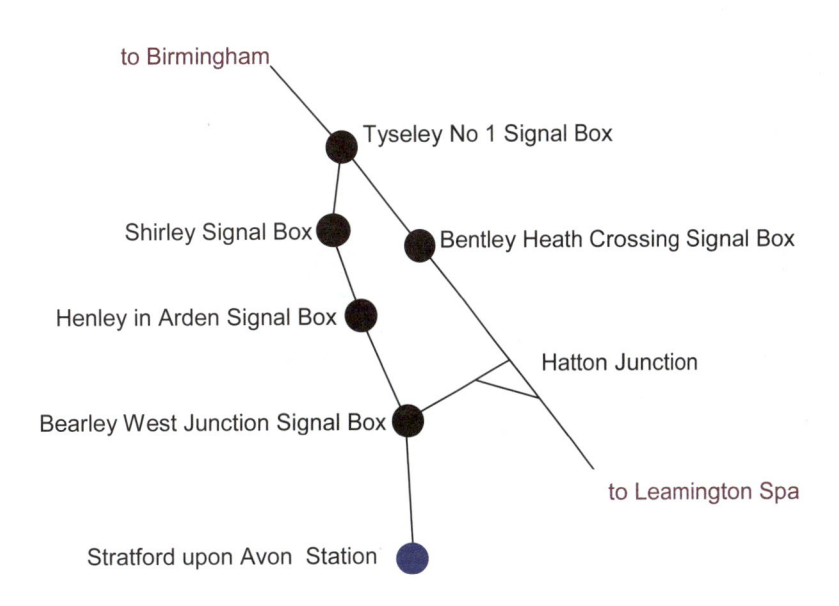

North Warwickshire

Fig. 209 is a very much simplified schematic to show what mechanical signalling and its infrastructure was like in later years. 'Was' is the operative word, as within the last few years it has mostly gone. The only survivor on the list is Tyseley No. 1, which controls a yard there and not running lines.

Birmingham and its environs was a massive hub of stations, goods depots, private sidings and even private railways to service the manufacturing colossus. Although the West Midlands could be thought of as the headquarters of the car industry, it manufactured everything from locks to nails to chains to jewellery and much more.

One signal box alone from the scores in the Birmingham district had 224 levers – and this was only the GWR; the LNWR and Midland Railway had a massive presence too.

The North Warwickshire line was a haven of peace from all this activity and the signal boxes depicted had more to do with the better-heeled commuters who needed to get into the city every day than the steam and sweat of the factories. North Warwickshire is pleasantly undulating farmland and of course it is the county of William Shakespeare.

Bentley Heath Crossing

Date Built	1932
GWR Type or Builder	GWR Type 28B+
No. of Levers	Nil (49)
Way of Working	Gate box only
Current Status	Demolished March 2008
Listed (Y/N)	N

Although the North Warwickshire line is thought of as running from Stratford-upon-Avon to Tyseley, Bentley Heath Crossing has been included in this section as it was geographically close.

Fig. 210 shows the front of the box, and one striking thing is that there is no short identifier plate as with all the other boxes so far. As it is only a gate box, supervising a level crossing, perhaps it was not thought to be important enough. Furthermore, the box did not appear on the master lists of signal boxes.

However, with sympathetically updated windows and original nearly everything else, the

Fig. 210 Bentley Heath Crossing signal box, March 2005.

box was an icon of a past era. As the box was a gate box, there was no frame fitted later, although there had been a 49-lever frame in there at some point. This means that the inside is not as important as the outside and, happily, thanks to the footbridge outside, the outside has been photographed more than most.

The box is similar to Abergavenny although much larger – and one wonders why, as Bentley Heath Crossing never had as many levers as Abergavenny.

Fig. 211 shows the door entrance to the staircase leading up to the operating room on the first floor. The frame room windows are the same front and back and the toilet block has been tacked on to the back.

The patch in the roof in Fig. 212 dates from the coal stove being taken away. When pot-bellied stoves were introduced there was no longer need for a chimney stack or fireplace and so timber boxes were popular in the cash-strapped 1930s. It was thought they would last ten to thirty years at the time. The box still has a slate roof though and terracotta ridge tiles with the cowl ventilators flashed on top.

The *raison d'être* of the box is below at the left with the crossing barriers. There had been four running lines past the box at one time but now only two and the buffer stops of the headshunt of the Dorridge station engineer's siding. Fig. 213 goes over the footbridge for a close-up of the terracotta ridge tile at the roof end, which looks like a strong wind would have it airborne. Fig. 214 gives a close-up view of the elusive cowl ventilators.

Knowle and Dorridge station was the scene of a serious fatal incident in August 1963 when an express train from Birmingham ran into goods wagons that were being shunted on the main line. It was a failure to warn Bentley Heath Signal box of

Fig. 211 Bentley Heath Crossing signal box side and rear detail, March 2005.

Fig. 212 Bentley Heath Crossing signal box roof detail, March 2005.

Fig. 213 Bentley Heath Crossing signal box, detail of roof ridge tiles, March 2005.

Fig. 214 Bentley Heath Crossing signal box roof ventilators detail, March 2005.

this line blockage that led to the collision. The line had, by this time, passed to the London Midland Region of British Railways.

An express hurtles past the box southbound in Fig. 215. Note the gaps where the other two tracks were, the goods loops at Dorridge station in the distance and the engineer's siding headshunt buffers slowly disappearing under the growth.

Fig. 216 offers a front detail. Note the original cast iron name plate in view and the fact that the locking frame windows are sliders, as are the operating room windows. You can also clearly see the lap-type timber construction.

Bearley West Junction (BJ)

Date Built	1907
GWR Type or Builder	GWR Type 7D+
No. of Levers	30
Way of Working	AB
Current Status	Demolished 2010
Listed (Y/N)	N

Fig. 215 Bentley Heath Crossing signal box with express heading towards Leamington Spa, March 2005.

Fig. 216 Bentley Heath Crossing signal box front detail, March 2005.

Fig. 217 Bearley West Junction signal box front detail, March 2005.

Bearley West Junction, or Bearley Junction as it later appeared, controlled the lines from Tyseley in the north and Hatton Junction in the east, the latter being single track. This has been London Midland Region territory so nearly all the signals are upper quadrant. The box was 17 miles and 61 chains (28.6km) from Tyseley South Junction.

Fig. 217 depicts the original cast iron name plate, which remained after the box's name had been changed. The soffits under the roof eaves appear to have been changed, or someone has put plastic ventilators in there; it looks like the former. A conscious effort has been made with the replacement windows to retain the GWR three over two windowpane style. The locking frame windows look similarly convincing. In the distance a signal arm is pulled OFF for a train from Stratford-upon-Avon towards Birmingham.

A closer view of the Stratford-upon-Avon part of the junction is shown in Fig. 218. The line to Stratford is beyond the home signal, which is on its own. To the right the line goes towards Birmingham, and towards the reader to Hatton Junction. At Hatton Junction there is a connection back up towards Birmingham but the main thrust of the junction is towards Leamington Spa.

Fig. 219 is a detail of the point rodding coming out of the frame room and the distinctive brickwork.

In Fig. 220 you can see the Birmingham line curving away in a long shot of the contrasting signalling styles. On the left is a lower quadrant steam-age GWR pattern home signal and on the right the rear of a London Midland upper quadrant with a sighting board that may also be used as a cricket sight screen.

Fig. 218 Bearley West Junction, looking towards Stratford-upon-Avon, March 2005.

Fig. 219 Bearley West Junction signal box front lower detail, March 2005.

Fig. 220 Bearley West Junction signal box upper and lower quadrant signals on the way to Birmingham, March 2005.

Fig. 221 Bearley West Junction signal box, Stratford line starter signal, March 2005.

Fig. 221 shows the inner home signal guarding the junction from the line coming from Hatton Junction. There is no disc plate to say where the signal belongs. Note the bullhead track and the more modern train protection warning system (TPWS) grid on the sleepers inside the 'four foot'.

Henley-in-Arden (HA)

Date Built	1907
GWR Type or Builder	GWR Type 7d
No. of Levers	57
Way of Working	AB
Current Status	Demolished 2010
Listed (Y/N)	N

Henley-in-Arden is a delightful English country town established about 900 years ago but given continued prosperity by commuters to Birmingham, thanks mainly to the railway.

The signal box, like so many others, once controlled more than the current layout: for many years there was a branch line to Alcester and this was part of the reason there were three platforms here originally. The signal box in Fig. 222 seems to have the same window treatment as others on the line but no ventilators. The cast name plate is another survivor of older times. The London Midland region upper quadrant signal is expecting a train from the Birmingham direction. Not only is it bullhead rail here but the permanent way gang have taken to painting the ends of check rails and wing rails white.

Henley-in-Arden general layout is shown in Fig. 223, with the GWR Edwardian station building in place, complete with chimney. These

Fig. 222 Henley-in-Arden signal box, November 2004.

station buildings with the triangular-shaped roof ends were very popular across the GWR for small to medium-sized stations. There are examples at Toddington on the Gloucestershire and Warwickshire Railway (G&WR), Bicester North and High Wycombe.

The footbridge spans more than two tracks as there were three platforms here. The footbridge has been removed since the picture was taken and presented to the Gloucestershire and Warwickshire Railway for their re-creation of Broadway station in Worcestershire.

Next is the view from that footbridge (Fig. 224). You can just see the beginnings of the siding with run-round loop on the left. Tended gardens have been part of the railway story since earliest days and someone is having a go here, but it is likely to be local people caring for their station rather than station staff, as most stations are not now staffed, or only at peak times.

Fig. 225 shows the signals to exit the siding and loop over where platform 3 was.

Fig. 223 Henley-in-Arden station and general layout, November 2004.

Fig. 224 Henley-in-Arden station and general layout from the footbridge, November 2004.

Shirley (SH)

Date Built	1907
GWR Type or Builder	GWR Type 7d
No. of Levers	31
Way of Working	AB
Current Status	Demolished 2010
Listed (Y/N)	N

Shirley is a suburb of Solihull, perhaps the most prosperous town in the West Midlands. Its wealth is mainly based on the Land Rover works in the town.

The signal box was closed and demolished after a good deal of local opposition, including from local politicians.

Fig. 226 depicts a signal box that is clearly cared for. The locking room window plating-over appears to be a more modern security precaution rather than a wartime brick-up measure. This is the first signal box on a platform, and we can see the arrangement of how the point rodding and signal wires are led out from under the platform. Note the GWR 'spear' fencing. This was solid steel or wrought iron with a hammered spear on the ends. It was supplied in prefabricated sections all ready to lay and secure to the ground. It is a wonder it has survived this long as a good deal of iron fencing railings were cut down to assist the war effort during World War II. There is now a modern replica that is plastic-coated.

Fig. 225 Henley-in-Arden station siding and loop starters, November 2004.

Fig. 226 Shirley signal box, April 2005.

Fig. 227 is a close-up view of how the rodding and signal wires are distributed and the massive girder needed to support the platform masonry. Wires are fed along the platform faces with pulleys secured to the platform wall.

The way to Birmingham is the focus of Fig. 228 with plenty of spear fencing and replica gas lamps. The outer home is OFF for a class 150 that is due. Note the ground disc is track circuited. Refuge siding could hold a two-car DMU but doesn't seem to get any use.

The class 150 has arrived (Fig. 229), bound for Snow Hill. Note the Edwardian GWR station buildings in GWR colours and the period footbridge.

Finally at Shirley, Fig. 230, looking towards Stratford-upon-Avon, is the view from the GWR footbridge with trailing crossover, unplated starter signal and track-circuited disc. The crossover looks well used so there may be trains terminating here from Birmingham.

Fig. 227 Shirley signal box rodding and signal wire, April 2005.

Fig. 228 (left) Shirley station looking towards Birmingham, April 2005.

Fig. 229 Shirley station, with a class 150 headed for Snow Hill, April 2005.

Fig. 230 Shirley station looking towards Stratford-upon-Avon, April 2005.

Tyseley No. 1 (TY1)

Date Built	1949
GWR Type or Builder	GWR Type 14
No. of Levers	30
Way of Working	TCB
Current Status	Active
Listed (Y/N)	N

Tyseley is the middle of a rolling stock yard and this is what it controls. The main running lines outside the yard are controlled by Saltley Power Signal Box soon to be West Midlands area ROC and the box works TCB to the control centre. It would appear that the only reason Tyseley No. 1 has escaped the two previous modernizations on the running lines outside the box is the fact that its function is solely contained within the local depot.

Figure 231 is a view from the nearby Tyseley Locomotive Works. This box has far more workaday appearance and less has been done than in other cases to retain the essential character of the box, perhaps in view of its location this is not surprising. The windows are of the single pane type and are 'whited' out halfway down. The name board is a modern printed plate on the end of the box. The roof is a corrugated iron type painted white which would certainly make it visible to a police helicopter. However from the World War II years onwards corrugated materials were used a lot, an example of this is Moreton on Lugg near Hereford. The yard siding exit has a 3ft arm, which is plated as TY1 28 and appears to be the signal to let Tyseley Locomotive Works trains out of their yard. In GWR days this signal would have had a ring on the arm to denote a goods or loop line function.

The three other siding exit signals behind TY1 28 are all upper quadrant subsidiary arms.

Fig. 232 shows Tyseley yard and box with a view of the multiplicity of lines in the area of the preserved line. This was once home to a double roundhouse and an allocation of 114 steam locomotives. One of the turntables has survived but not the shed buildings. There are a whole host of modern buildings housing the locomotive works.

Tyseley yard and a lone lower quadrant home signal with a 4ft arm appear at Fig. 233. Note the

Fig. 231   Tyseley No. 1 signal box and yard exit home signal, September 2006.

Fig. 232   Tyseley No. 1 signal box and yard, September 2006.

Fig. 233 Tyseley No. 1 signal box home signal and GWR point levers, September 2006.

Fig. 234 Tyseley Warwick Road, Tyseley Locomotive Works, September 2006.

GWR point levers painted yellow and the ends of checkrails and wingrails on points painted yellow.

Tyseley Warwick Road signal box has been reconstructed on the Tyseley Locomotive Works site nearby (Fig. 234). This was erected in 1980 and was previously at Holesmouth Junction in the docks complex at Bristol. St Andrew's Junction later on in the book was a neighbour.

Worcester to Birmingham

Fig. 235 is a schematic diagram depicting the line from Worcester to Birmingham, which fringes to Droitwich Spa, as Worcester itself has been covered elsewhere. Leaving the industrial and populous West Midlands behind, the countryside of north Worcestershire is pleasantly undulating, passing through Britain's one-time carpet capital of Kidderminster to more pastoral scenes and towards the fruit-growing areas of the county.

Change has arrived and some of the signal boxes depicted here are no longer with us.

Droitwich Spa (DS)

Date Built	1907
GWR Type or Builder	GWR Type 7d+
No. of Levers	79
Way of Working	AB, TCB
Current Status	Active
Listed (Y/N)	N

Droitwich has existed since Roman times, and in early days it was discovered that there were extraordinarily large deposits of salt underground. It

Fig. 235   Birmingham–Worcester line schematic diagram of mechanical signal boxes.

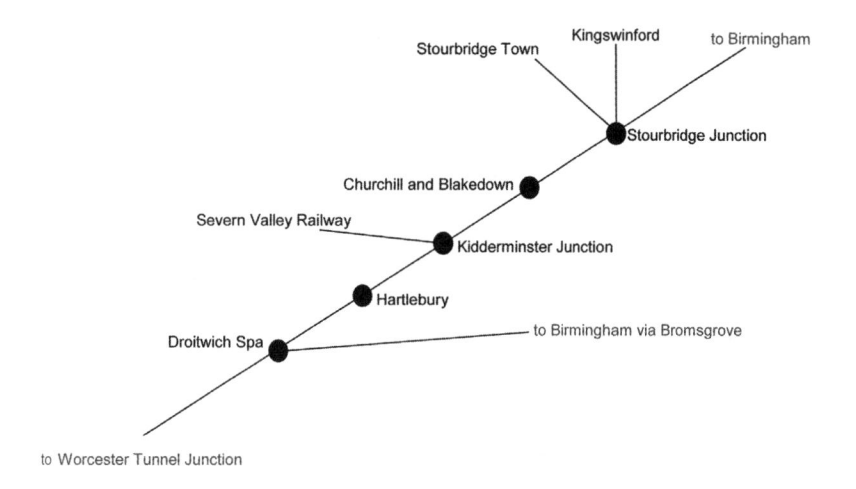

Fig. 236   Droitwich Spa signal box, July 2014.

Fig. 237   Droitwich Spa signal box from the station car park, July 2014.

produces a brine solution with ten times the saltiness of sea water, so although it is not drinkable, it was used for bathing. Not only that, but the brine springs are warm although not up to body temperature. This ensured that Droitwich became a spa town and was particularly popular in the nineteenth century after the railway arrived. In addition, partly due to the salt in the earth, Droitwich became famous as the long-wave transmitting station of the BBC. Its broadcasts would be listened to clandestinely by people in the occupied countries in Europe in World War II.

Droitwich Spa signal box is similar to Henley-in-Arden but has a larger lever frame (Fig. 236). The box is situated in the V of a junction and is bounded by the Droitwich canal on one side and the River Salwarpe on the other. It works AB to Worcester Tunnel Junction, AB to Kidderminster Junction and TCB to Gloucester Power signal box for the Bromsgrove direction. This latter route connects with the former Midland Railway main line and the Lickey Incline, the steepest main-line gradient in Britain.

The box looks a bit careworn now as it has lost its cast name plate in the last ten years, and two of the four ventilators have gone. Despite plain-paned main windows, the locking frame windows appear original.

Fig. 238   General layout of Droitwich Spa signal box and tracks and signals, July 2014.

Droitwich Spa signal box appears to be sitting back on its heels, so to speak, in Fig. 237: this kind of minor subsidence on what has been made-up ground in the first place is quite common after about a hundred years in service. The GWR planted not only pine trees at their stations but also buddleia, so perhaps that is a GWR buddleia in the foreground. The pine trees were so that passengers could spot the station in the middle of nowhere, which quite a few of them were. It also provided a bit of foliage and shelter in winter.

Droitwich Spa signal box and its immediate environs from the station footbridge are shown in Fig. 238. The route to Birmingham via Kidderminster is on the left and the route to Stoke Junction, which is the connection to the Midland main line, is on the right. Although the latter appears to be double track it goes into single track about half a mile from the box. Note the double line catch point in the down left-hand side Kidderminster track, in the far left of the picture. If a train is derailed intentionally here it would take out the point rodding and bracket signal but this is preferable to a collision.

Fig. 239   Droitwich Spa station, January 2004.

Fig. 240   Limit of shunt indicator outside Droitwich Spa station, January 2004.

Fig. 241   Up platform starter signal at Droitwich Spa station, January 2004.

Fig. 242   Class 172 DMU slowing down for Droitwich Spa station, July 2014.

The down goods loop doesn't appear to get much trade although the up goods loop, past the signal box to the left, is used and also has a tail lamp camera. A train is signalled to arrive from Kidderminster.

Fig. 239 shows the view towards the signal box and junction ten years earlier. The class 150 is Kidderminster bound and the signaller has replaced the platform starter and bracket signal behind the train but not the down main starter, signal DS15 in the distance, as the train hasn't passed it yet. Note the home signal coming off the Kidderminster line to the left is on the left-hand side of the picture and is much taller than its later replacement in Fig. 238. Note also the centre-balanced platform starters for the down main and the down goods loop.

On the way to Worcester, a limit of shunt indicator (Fig. 240) from the steam age allows a train to proceed up a line so far under the visual supervision of the signaller but it has not been signalled nor does it have permission to continue into the next block section.

Droitwich Spa station up platform starter to Worcester, signal DS70, is shown in Fig. 241. The post is shorter than usual as the signal would have to be sighted through the gap left by the road overbridge in Fig. 239.

Back to busy, more recent times at Droitwich Spa station, as a class 172 DMU arrives from Kidderminster and another train is signalled for Kidderminster (Fig. 242).

Fig. 243 is another view of Droitwich Spa station, with the centre-balanced arms on the bracket as platform starters.

Fig. 243   Droitwich Spa station with starter signals, July 2014

Finally at Droitwich Spa there is another home signal (Fig. 244) and although not apparently plated, it is believed to be DS74, up intermediate home coming from Kidderminster.

Hartlebury (HY)

Date Built	1876
GWR Type or Builder	Mackenzie and Holland Type 2 (GWR)
No. of Levers	IFS Panel
Way of Working	AB
Current Status	Demolished *c.* August 2012
Listed (Y/N)	N

Hartlebury Castle not only had a GWR Castle class express passenger locomotive named after it but was the fortified home of the bishops of Worcester. The local preservation trust is engaged in trying to buy the estate from the Church Commissioners. It is an extraordinarily diverse building with a rich array of treasures within. The ecclesiastical theme is apparent.

Hartlebury was also home to an RAF maintenance unit that specialized in the storage of aircraft spares during World War II. It closed in 1975 and is now an industrial estate.

Just north of where the box was sited was the junction with what has become known as the Severn Valley Railway. Together with the junction from Kidderminster, this made a triangle of lines that had an apex at Bewdley.

Fig. 244   Outer home signal, Droitwich Spa, July 2014.

Fig. 245   Hartlebury signal box, January 2006.

Fig. 246   Hartlebury signal box, side and rear view, January 2006.

Fig. 247 Hartlebury original station building, January 2006.

Fig. 248 Hartlebury station looking towards Droitwich Spa, January 2006.

Hartlebury signal box in Worcestershire was another of the early Mackenzie and Holland of Worcester products and was in the top ten of early survivors. Boxes before 1870 are almost unknown because the railways became obliged, after various gruesome accidents, to change their systems to 'lock block and brake' from almost anything. So these 1870s signal boxes were the harbingers of the modern railway and were basically safe – and proved it for almost 150 years. Any mechanical device can be defeated and it was these subsequent accidents that hastened the arrival of automation.

The box shown in Fig. 245 had retained locking room windows and had an array of cast iron strengtheners to stop the front wall from bulging out. Note there's only one signaller leaning-out bar across one window.

The side and rear are shown in Fig. 246. Note the chimney stack on the box wall, pot insulators from another age for external communications. There is no cast iron name plate here, just a printed out self-adhesive strip. No toilet block has been tacked on here, so the building next to the signaller's car could be a Portaloo or similar.

Fig. 247 shows Hartlebury station on the down platform, looking towards Droitwich Spa. The original station building is being developed into a restaurant and microbrewery – note its bus shelter replacement along the platform.

The view in Fig. 248 is towards Droitwich Spa. On the down and up side track you can see a pair of heritage bullhead rails in the 'four foot'. These are used to hold the adjacent track sections together when it becomes necessary to join two sections of continually welded track with an expansion joint. The rail should be able to expand and move in the joint but the sleepers should not be going anywhere. There is also a train protection and warning system (TPWS) grid nearby on the down nearest side.

Fig. 249 Hartlebury station looking towards Birmingham, January 2006.

Fig. 250   Hartlebury box and crossing, January 2006.

Fig. 249 looks towards Birmingham. The box's sole point work, the trailing crossover, can be seen, as well as the crossing. The platforms here are quite short and that prevents a good many other trains from stopping here. Nevertheless there are still thirteen trains a day that stop here. Stations such as these have become commuter hubs in recent years and consequently witnessed a dramatic increase in usage. Despite seeing a temporary fall-off in passenger numbers in 2010–12, the usage is six times what it was ten years previously.

The final view of Hartlebury signal box (Fig. 250) shows the Severn Valley junction on the left past the box.

Kidderminster Junction (KJ)

Date Built	1953
GWR Type or Builder	BR, WR Type 16+
No. of Levers	66
Way of Working	AB (at survey)
Current Status	Demolished December 2012
Listed (Y/N)	N

Kidderminster Junction was so called because it was one of the connecting points of what is now the Severn Valley Railway. There is still a connection with the SVR but no regular through service and the line terminates at Bridgnorth rather than Shrewsbury as originally. Kidderminster station had a charming half-timbered station building that was unique. It was demolished in 1968, before English Heritage got off the ground with respect to railway buildings, otherwise it would probably have been listed, like the Doric arch at Euston station should have been.

Kidderminster also had an engine shed and a massive goods shed, and no doubt many miles of carpet were sent off to customers from here. For about 100 years the railway was the only practical way to move goods around the country for any distance.

The goods shed is now the carriage workshops of the Severn Valley Railway. The former engine

Fig. 251   Kidderminster Junction signal box, August 2006.

shed, which had housed sixteen steam locomotives, was sited on what is now SVR property, opposite the new carriage sheds there.

The signal box has ultimately fared no better than the station in that it was demolished in 2012. There was a movement to have it listed but this was rejected. It had some merit architecturally and was unusual although perhaps for traditional signalling aficionados it might have been an acquired taste, with a bit too much Festival of Britain (1951) about it.

Control has passed to Saltley power box in Birmingham. The points have been converted to electro-hydraulic operation and signals are colour light, operating under TCB.

Fig. 251 is a general view of the box looking towards Droitwich Spa. We are back in London Midland Region territory again, and the signals are all upper quadrant, including the ground discs, one of which is on stilts. The crossover just to the right of the box is a turnback siding used to temporarily store a train before setting off back in the same direction from which it arrived. However, the crossover is simply a headshunt that terminates in a sand drag. We have not seen this before but it is a device to slow the progress of runaway vehicles rather than just derail them, as you would have with trap or catch points. Perhaps this feature has some roots in history as a freight train demolished the original GWR signal box in 1937.

When the replacement box was recently demolished its frame was a GWR original, and that frame has now been donated to the Severn Valley Railway across the tracks in the foreground.

Fig. 252 is looking the other way, towards Birmingham. The up home signal appears to be a Western Region bracket with ex-GWR-type finial but an upper quadrant arm, so is a real mix. The three sidings no longer have a running line connection and the work to sever those looks recent – the photograph is from August 2006. The siding nearest the running lines has had its buffer stops removed.

The up platform of the rudimentary station can also be seen in the distance. The point in the foreground on the left is the connection to the Severn

Fig. 252   Kidderminster Junction bracket signal and severed sidings, August 2006.

Fig. 253   Kidderminster Junction signal box from the down platform and GWR goods shed, August 2006.

Valley Railway. As part of the works for the conversion of the line to TCB and closure of the box, a crossover was put in to connect the right-hand running line with the SVR.

On the station up platform (Fig. 253) a train to Droitwich Spa is due, as the two up home signals in the picture are OFF. The box is beyond the overbridge in the distance.

Fig. 254   Kidderminster Junction and GWR goods shed with up home signal, August 2006.

Fig. 255   Kidderminster Junction signal box through the Severn Valley Railway yard, August 2006.

The massive structure on the right is the former GWR goods shed, now the SVR carriage workshops. The SVR has several sets of vintage carriages that are now seen as a national treasure and much time, effort and cash has gone into their restoration and protection in the newer carriage sheds across the SVR tracks.

Fig. 254 includes another GWR tubular post and bracket and finial with an LMR upper quadrant arm. Note the way the disconnected siding ends up at the end of the platform ramp. The old goods shed still has a Great Western Railway painted sign on the gable ends, much like the example we saw at Worcester. There are also other examples at Stroud and Wrexham General.

The final view of Kidderminster Junction is from the SVR yard (Fig. 255), with a cash register signal and others, and a fine replica GWR box with Kidderminster Junction in the background beyond the overbridge.

Churchill and Blakedown (BN)

Date Built	1881
GWR Type or Builder	GWR Type 4c
No. of Levers	–
Way of Working	AB
Current Status	Dismantled 2013
Listed (Y/N)	N

Like its near neighbour at Hagley, Blakedown has its own stately home in Harborough Hall. Where the two villages are dissimilar is that Hagley station has survived almost untouched and Blakedown is the two platforms with bus shelters model. The station was originally called Churchill, as that was the parish name, and became Churchill and Blakedown later. Later still it is referred to as just Blakedown. On news of its closure the parish council felt there was enough support to save the signal box from demolition and, with Network Rail's help, the signal box was dismantled for re-erection in the village a short way from the line. The ex-GWR locomotive

Fig. 256   Churchill and Blakedown signal box, March 2004.

120

Hagley Hall is currently at Bridgnorth on the Severn Valley Railway undergoing restoration after a twenty-seven-year retirement. Although nearby Hagley station has no signal box it has a GWR footbridge that is Grade II listed.

Churchill and Blakedown signal box was measured as being 138 miles and 51 chains (223.1km) from Paddington via Didcot, Oxford and Worcester. These measurements were made on the traditional quarter-mile posts going back to the nineteenth century and are still in use today. However, it was just over 3 miles (5km) from Kidderminster Junction. The box supervised a level crossing and was an intermediate block post working AB to Kidderminster Junction and Stourbridge Junction.

Fig. 256 depicts the box in 2004. It contained an individual function switch (IFS) panel to control the colour light signals and crossover and barriers. The block bell and instrument functions were usually integrated into the panel. This was AB working modernized. There were a few loose slates on the porch roof but otherwise it was in reasonable condition.

It is easy to see why the villagers were reluctant to let the box be demolished as it had been part of the village scene for so many years (Fig. 257). The station is enjoying a renaissance passenger-wise and is well established on the Birmingham commuter run. With the exception of a couple of blips, the passenger numbers have trebled in ten years.

The side and rear of the box in Fig. 258 show the familiar lookout window at the rear to keep an eye on the traffic, as it is the signaller who operates the barriers. The iron rod across the window at the rear is missing or has been adapted to do something else by the look of it. The original chimney stack is present and only the pot is missing.

Stourbridge Junction (SJ)

Date Built	1901
GWR Type or Builder	GWR Type 7b
No. of Levers	–
Way of Working	TCB, OTS
Current Status	Closed 2012
Listed (Y/N)	N

Stourbridge was a well-known centre for the glass-making industry, specializing in hand-blown and sculpted decorative products rather than the plate or float glasses used in the building industry. The trade was established in about 1600 and used the skills of French Huguenot miners. There were coal mines to hand and large deposits of the fireclay needed to line the kilns in which glass was smelted.

Fig. 257 Churchill and Blakedown signal box from the crossing, March 2004.

Fig. 258 Churchill and Blakedown signal box, side and rear view, March 2004.

Fig. 259 Stourbridge Junction signal box and staircase, November 2008.

Fig. 260 Stourbridge Junction signal box, November 2008.

It was also a considerable railway junction, which is retained to some extent. There were extensive goods yards and sidings as well as a locomotive depot built by the GWR in 1926 in place of an inferior structure. In 1947 there were eighty-two locomotives allocated, mostly for shunting or local short-distance freight trains. The depot was one of the last GWR depots to remain open but closed in 1966. All others on the former Western Region had closed by the end of 1965 but a few lasted longer as they had been hived onto the London Midland Region in 1963. At present a train depot is still at Stourbridge Junction in the form of a Chiltern Trains depot, which is off the down goods loop.

The main part of Stourbridge Junction is the junction of the lines to Walsall, Kingswinford and the lines to Smethwick and Snow Hill station, Birmingham. The line to Walsall was closed off with stop blocks through lack of use except to a private siding for Tata steel. There is now talk of a tram system using the Walsall line.

The Kingswinford branch was to a steel stockholder and London and Cambridge Properties, and that would appear to be out of use now. The only traffic this branch now sees is the traffic from Llanwern and Port Talbot to the Tata steel terminal at Round Oak.

The final branch of the junction is to Stourbridge Town station. The branch is reputed to be the shortest in Europe at only 50 chains, or just over half a mile (1km) in length. The original station building at Town was constructed in the French style, similar to Wrexham General, but fared no better than Kidderminster and was demolished in 1977.

Until recently there had been class 150 DMUs single-car units used on the branch but the branch went greener when it started using the Parry Peoplemover. This is a light railcar-type vehicle

Fig. 261 Stourbridge Junction station with Stourbridge Town platform on the left, September 2014.

that uses stored energy in a flywheel for propulsion and control. There is a small depot for these vehicles at Stourbridge Junction.

In Fig. 259 Stourbridge Junction can be seen as a fine figure of a signal box. Unofficial means of assessing size tells us that this is big, with five ventilator cowls, eclipsing anything seen thus far. It still has its original cast name plate of Stourbridge Junction Middle Signal Box. The windows have a pleasing original appearance but the locking frame windows are bricked up as a blast damage precaution. The gap at the bottom of the front wall suggests a mass of point rodding coming out when it was done mechanically.

There were originally seven boxes with Stourbridge in the title and Stourbridge Junction had ninety-one levers, which does not seem many for such a big box.

The signal box is seen from the Birmingham end in Fig. 260. The air conditioner doesn't seem large enough for the operating floor, as if it's a standard, one-size-fits-all unit.

Stourbridge Junction is a standard GWR structure for through/junction stations (Fig. 261). Note there is an early GWR platform seat. The branch to Stourbridge Town is on the left and there is a connection to the main running lines from the point at the end of the platform. This point is now the only lever-worked device in the area and is worked from a ground frame.

The ground frame is situated just at the Kidderminster end of the box, and you can just

Fig. 262 Stourbridge Junction ground frame, September 2014.

see the blue lever of a facing point lock as the point carries passengers over it (Fig. 262). The rodding goes away to the point on the left.

In Fig. 263 the ground frame and rodding show up, as does a catch point that would derail a train going into the Stourbridge Town platform. There are also two notices, one about the class 139 Peoplemover and the other about the end of OTS working. There are two class 139s and they need to be rotated on a regular basis. The point at the end of the platform allows one unit to run up towards the catch point and stop and the other to emerge from the shed at the end of the Stourbridge Town platform. The points are then changed and the exchange unit runs up the branch a short way. The unit standing near the catch point can then run back into the shed. Thus the change is

Fig. 263 Stourbridge Junction station and end of OTS section, September 2014.

Fig. 264   Stourbridge Junction station and Parry Peoplemover, class 139, September 2014.

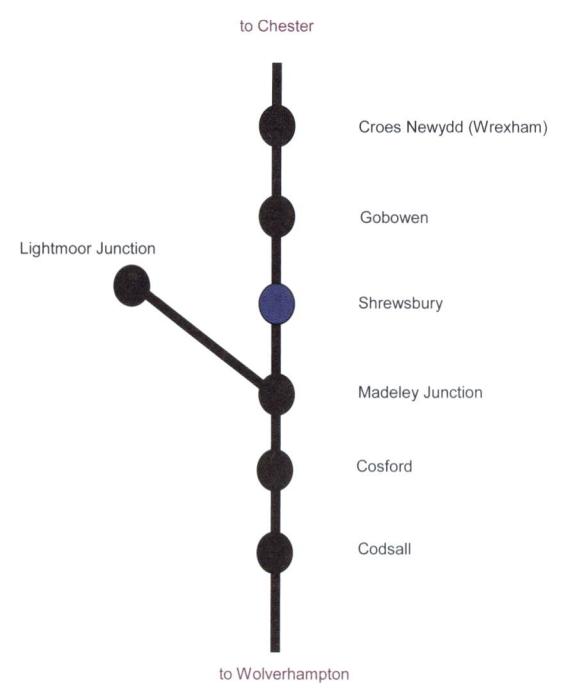

Fig. 265   Chester–Wolverhampton line schematic diagram of mechanical signal boxes.

effected. Note the class 172 DMU heading for Snow Hill, Birmingham and the colour light signal with 'feather' or route indicator. Beyond the box on the left is the Traincare depot.

Finally at Stourbridge, Fig. 264 shows the class 139 Parry Peoplemover ready to set off for Stourbridge Town. The shed where they are kept is on the extreme left.

Chester to Wolverhampton

Fig. 265 is a schematic diagram depicting the line. It originally ran from Wolverhampton Low Level on the GWR, but after the line was taken over by the London Midland Region of BR, Low Level was closed and lay derelict for many years. The station building was Grade II listed in 1987 and has survived; after numerous plans it was last proposed to be converted into a banqueting hall.

The line runs through some fairly industrial and densely populated urban areas in the south, changing to rural Shropshire then heading into Wales, where the backdrop is pleasant hillsides and valleys, before running through the River Dee plain to Chester. The line from Wrexham to Chester had been converted to single track and has just been re-doubled.

Codsall (CL)

Date Built	1929
GWR Type or Builder	GWR Type 28+
No. of Levers	25
Way of Working	AB
Current Status	Preserved off-site
Listed (Y/N)	Y

Codsall is a neat village near Wolverhampton and the station is much cherished and a credit to the local people. The station building proper is a restaurant and has a fine GWR footbridge dating to 1883, though this was badly damaged by contractors working at the station just after the survey in 2005. It has been repaired.

The signal box was made redundant in the 2006 re-signalling of the area and, as it is a listed building, was presented to the Dean Forest Railway,

Fig. 266   Codsall signal box and track layout near Wolverhampton, April 2004.

Fig. 267   Codsall signal box, April 2004.

who are planning to use it at their Whitemoor station.

Fig. 266, from the road overbridge, is a general view of the simplest of layouts, with just a trailing crossover to mar the arrow-straight main line at this point. The box was 146 miles and 26 chains (235.5km) from Paddington via Oxford and Snow Hill station and the view is towards Shrewsbury and the north. It was about 5 miles (8km) north of Wolverhampton. The signals are a mixture of London Midland posts and signal arms and Western Region posts with finials and London Midland arms. The small yellow post this side of the signal box is a quarter-mile marker post, and variations on these would include the mileage as given above but to the quarter mile. On the opposite side of the track is the signaller's car and a walkway across to the box.

The two semaphores in view appear to be motor operated and that may be something to do with returning the signals to danger automatically after a train has passed. We have seen some of this already at Craven Arms. The box only has a few months left in service at this point.

Fig. 267 zooms in a little closer and reveals a modernized box with windows sympathetic to the originals but no cowl ventilators. The slate roof with terracotta ridge tiles is present as at Bentley Heath Crossing, with which this box was contemporary. The internal staircase door has been left open.

Looking back up the line towards Wolverhampton from the station platform, Fig. 268 takes in the overbridge. The ballast is a prodigious depth here.

Fig. 269 offers a general view of the station at Codsall with the splendid 1883 footbridge, blissfully unaware that it will soon be never quite the

Fig. 268   Codsall signal box and track layout looking towards Wolverhampton, April 2004.

Fig. 269 Codsall restored station before the bridge was damaged by a contractor, April 2004.

same again. A contractor's digger all but destroyed the bridge; and though it has been restored, it now sits somewhat higher to fit in with current regulations. The station building is an award-winning pub and restaurant with lots of railway memorabilia on display. The cast iron bridge on the left is also attractively restored. The lamps are later but at least have a finial to be in keeping.

Cosford (CD)

Date Built	1939
GWR Type or Builder	GWR Type 12+
No. of Levers	39
Way of Working	AB
Current Status	Demolished 2007
Listed (Y/N)	N

Cosford is just over a mile from Albrighton station so would seem to be superfluous. Albrighton station is still original to a remarkable degree and now some of it is listed.

However, nearby RAF Cosford was seen as a key place for the training of airmen needed to work on the aircraft that would help fight World War II. This led to the establishment of No. 2 School of Technical Training. There was also an airfield and a hospital. (The hospital was later made available to NHS patients and was well thought of by people in the area until it closed in 1977.)

This meant there was a need to build a railway station adjacent to the camp. The camp itself was expanded, and while a good deal of it was wooden huts there was also the Fulton Block, which was a massive structure for its time.

The station platform and shelters are unusual in being wood, while the station building next to the rail overbridge is traditional brick. Like a lot of the buildings on this line, they have survived where the signal boxes have not. The layout includes two goods loops and a connection to RAF Cosford, which was used in later years to deliver coke for the central heating system. Subsequent to that, a track maintenance machine was stored there.

Although the box has been demolished, a good many of the fittings and fixtures were donated to the preservation movement.

Fig. 270 shows a view of the box and goods loops arrangements looking north towards Shrewsbury and Chester. What can just be seen is the entry to RAF Cosford just off the right-hand, up, goods loop. Although the signals are predominantly London Midland upper quadrants, the goods loop exit signals are lower quadrant. In common with other locations, the goods loop is not track circuited. Note the rail-built buffer stop of bullhead rail. Note also

Fig. 270 Cosford signal box and track layout, south Shropshire, April 2004. Note the RAF Cosford connection.

Fig. 271 Cosford signal box and track layout, south Shropshire, April 2004. Note the BR WR posts with LMR arms.

that there is a headshunt at the end of the loop rather than trap points, as a loco and train may be held there shunting into the RAF Cosford siding. Part of the training area of RAF Cosford is to the right and behind the signal box is the museum, which is on the airfield side of the camp.

Fig. 271 is still looking northwards, and here we have the down goods loop bracket signal. The platforms are built of timber on stilts and some of that construction can be seen on the down platform on the left. Note the catch points off the down goods loop.

Still looking northwards, Fig. 272 shows the platform construction and the wooden station waiting shelters, which are all original.

The rear of the box (Fig. 273) is partly built of brick – surprisingly, as one might have expected wood by this time as an economy measure. There is no chimney stack and the windows are good replacements, but the locking frames are the galvanized iron Crittall type that became popular with dwellings in the 1930s. They were part of the art deco style at the time, although the box is anything but. Those Crittall-type windows are shown

Fig. 272 Cosford station with wooden platforms and waiting room shelters, April 2004.

Fig. 273 Rear of Cosford signal box, April 2004. Note the RAF Cosford buildings behind.

Fig. 274   Cosford signal box locking room window and frame within, April 2004.

Madeley Junction (MJ)

Date Built	1969
GWR Type or Builder	London Midland Region Type 15+
No. of Levers	40
Way of Working	AB, TCB, KT
Current Status	Demolished November 2012
Listed (Y/N)	N

in more detail in Fig. 274, and you can just see the locking frame within.

Fig. 275 is back on the overbridge looking north, and you can see the bracket signal for the up goods loop. Note that the crossover is electrically worked. What looks like the tail fin of a Bristol Britannia in BOAC livery is visible in the museum.

Looking back towards Wolverhampton (Fig. 276), you can see the down goods loop on the right. The loops are not long enough for the coal trains going to and from Ironbridge power station so are no longer used.

The town of Madeley is now part of Telford but its origins go back to the eighth century. Within its boundaries is the UNESCO world heritage site of Ironbridge and what is commonly called the cradle of the industrial revolution. In terms of the manufacture of iron products it was certainly a forerunner and is still strong in manufacturing today. The Shropshire coalfield was worked very early and prominent but there is no coal mining there now.

The power station at Ironbridge needs to be fed with coal, however, and this was part of the reason for Madeley Junction signal box's existence. Not only was it the junction for Ironbridge but it was also the junction for a line to Wellington via Doseley and Horsehay, long since closed. The junction for both lines led off the single line and the line split up at a further junction down the line.

The box worked TCB to Wellington, which the box controlled, and fringed to Abbey Foregate at

Fig. 275   Cosford looking towards Shrewsbury, with the RAF Aerospace museum on the left, April 2004.

Fig. 276   Cosford signal box and track layout, with down goods loop signals, April 2004.

Fig. 277 Madeley Junction signal box and track layout, near Telford, September 2005.

Fig. 278 Madeley Junction signal box and track layout, including single slip, September 2005.

Shrewsbury. It worked AB to Cosford and KT on the single line to Lightmoor Junction towards Ironbridge. Later on the box controlled the sections at Cosford and Codsall but it too succumbed eventually. Instead of levers or panels the extra area was covered with a Westcad VDU using solid state or electronic interlocking.

Fig. 277 reveals the box was a standard 1950s LM Region product. The tracks at the front and on the right are the main line and we are looking towards Shrewsbury. The track on the left is the branch to Ironbridge and the path taken by the coal trains referred to in the section on Cosford above. The branch to Ironbridge is actually a loop of up and down tracks that join up after about 30 chains only – less than half a mile. It enables one train to be held 'in the loop' while still being able to admit another to the branch. Clearly the train being held must have surrendered the key token before it is used for the second train.

Fig. 278 shows a fairly unusual piece of track kit now in the shape of the crossing in the foreground, which is a single slip. They used to be very common and can still be found at major stations. This is a switched crossing, which enables trains to either cross tracks as they would at an ordinary crossing, or, when the crossing is switched, to run from the bottom of the picture onto the branch to the left. You should be able to see that the crossing is not switched in the photograph – the blades are set to run towards Shrewsbury.

The long run of track leading up to the branch on the right is shown in Fig. 279. This is to enable a northbound train to use this line as a loop to run round the train via the crossing and loop seen at Fig. 278. This would enable the train to be stabled or parked off the main line whilst the manoeuvre was completed.

Fig. 279 Madeley Junction track layout crossover and approach road, September 2005.

Fig. 280 Lightmoor Junction signal box, near Telford, August 2008.

Fig. 281 Lightmoor Junction signal box, looking back towards Madeley Junction, August 2008.

Lightmoor Junction (LJ)

Date Built	1951
GWR Type or Builder	BR Western Region Type 15+
No. of Levers	31
Way of Working	KT and Telephone
Current Status	Closed in 2006; preserved by Telford Steam Railway
Listed (Y/N)	N

Lightmoor Junction originally provided a connection to Wellington, which was some junction in itself. It had lines to Crewe via Market Drayton and Nantwich as well as Stafford and Coalport, and its own engine shed, which closed in 1964.

Lightmoor Junction is another of those signal boxes that lost its junction but for operational reasons was kept open. It was originally the junction for a line to Wellington and this was via Horsehay, which is now the headquarters of the Telford Steam Railway, formerly the Horsehay Steam Trust. The TSR leased the signal box from Network Rail in 2008, two years after it closed as part of the same process that saw Codsall and Cosford lose their signal boxes.

The box worked key token to Madeley Junction and by telephone to the double track to Ironbridge power station. This line was singled and that removed the reason for Lightmoor Junction's existence.

Fig. 280 shows a fairly plain structure with bricked-up locking room windows and wire mesh grilles on the windows. Clearly these are security measures rather than air-raid precautions as we have seen elsewhere. The brickwork is quite pleasing and varied.

Fig. 282 Lightmoor Junction signal box token exchange platform, August 2008.

Fig. 281 offers a bargain deal for trespassers, as the current tariff is £1,000! This view is looking towards Madeley Junction.

The platform where the key token from Madeley Junction was retrieved and where the token was issued to those trains proceeding to Madeley Junction is shown in Fig. 282. Although the box is now out of commission the line remains well used, as can be seen from the shiny state of the rail in the foreground.

Gobowen North (GN)

Date Built	1884
GWR Type or Builder	Mackenzie and Holland Type 3 (GWR)
No. of Levers	16
Way of Working	AB
Current Status	Active
Listed (Y/N)	N

Gobowen is a pleasant village in north Shropshire and the one-time junction with the branch line to the market town of Oswestry and Cambrian Railways territory. The GWR had a station at Oswestry but that was converted into a goods depot when the GWR absorbed the Cambrian Railways. Trains from Gobowen then used the former Cambrian station. The line continued in use after the Oswestry end of the Cambrian was closed in 1966, as it serviced a number of quarries beyond Oswestry. The quarry traffic ceased in 1989 but the line has remained. A preservation group is hoping to restore services, and the Cambrian station building, signal box and some signalling at Oswestry are evidence of that.

Gobowen station building, on the down side, is an architectural gem and is Grade II listed. It was constructed in the Florentine or Italianate style in 1846 by the Shrewsbury and Chester Railway, a precursor to the GWR. There were originally two signal boxes at Gobowen, north and south. The south box was much larger and controlled the Oswestry branch as well as a group of sidings and a goods yard, but as north has the supervised crossing, it was retained and the south box closed. There is a freight working from Carlisle Kingmoor to the Kronospan chipboard factory at Chirk a few miles to the north of Gobowen. The trains head south and then do a massive loop in the West Midlands before resuming their journey north. This may have something to do with the Chester–Wrexham single to double track re-conversion.

Fig. 283 Gobowen North signal box, September 2014.

Looking at the box itself in Fig. 283, you can see it has modernized features such as windows and door but retains its Mackenzie and Holland corporate look. The cast name plate is possibly the reason it was not renamed when Gobowen South closed. Any functionality for the south of Gobowen is worked by a local panel there but the control to enable that is operated by the signaller at Gobowen North. This is rather like the ancillary north ground frame at Worcester we met earlier that has to be released by Shrub Hill box before it can be operated.

Looking at the rear of the box in Fig. 284, it has the usual lookout windows that traditional gate boxes have to keep an eye on the road traffic. A toilet block has been tacked on to the end.

A glance down the line towards Wrexham and Chester gives a glimpse of the outline of the Welsh hills in the distance that are only a few miles away

Fig. 284 Gobowen North signal box rear view, September 2014.

Fig. 285 Gobowen North signal box track layout towards Wrexham and Chester, September 2014.

now (Fig. 285). The signals are as at Dorrington, only with the up and down reversed in the sense that all up signals are lower quadrant and down signals upper quadrant. There is a trailing crossover with an LED lamp indicator rather than disc, although there is a disc the other side of the crossing.

We head back towards Shrewsbury and Wolverhampton in Fig. 286, and the motor-worked platform starter that we met in the motorized section (*see* Fig. 30). Beyond the GWR canopies on the right is the Oswestry branch and beyond that, in the far distance, an automatically operated colour light signal.

Fig. 287 is a closer view of the Oswestry branch connection, and from the top there is the beginning of a loop that soon goes to single track as you go further towards Oswestry to the right. Next is the main-line trailing connection, and the points there appear to be clipped and locked in position. After that is a headshunt for the two sidings that still run into the station, one of which could be a bay platform – there is an earlier view in Fig. 289 to show how it was.

Fig. 286 Gobowen station looking towards Shrewsbury, September 2014.

Fig. 287   Gobowen station and Oswestry branch connections, September 2014.

The Grade II listed station building is shown in Fig. 288, and to the left of that the overgrown bay and sidings referred to in Fig. 287.

Fig. 289 goes back to 2004, showing that the right-hand siding could be and was the bay platform for the Gobowen–Oswestry shuttle up to the 1960s. The coal merchant is no longer trading there and some of the yard land is up for sale at the time of writing. It is now rather a jungle but the track is still there.

We say goodbye to Gobowen with a shot of a class 158 DMU disappearing over the gradient towards Shrewsbury – as it passes the colour light signal, the signal is changed to red automatically (Fig. 290).

Croes Newydd North Fork (CN)

Date Built	1905 (estimated)
GWR Type or Builder	GWR Type 27c+
No. of Levers	83 before frame removal
Way of Working	AB, TCB
Current Status	Active
Listed (Y/N)	N

Fig. 288   Gobowen station in the Florentine style, September 2014.

Fig. 289   Gobowen station bay platform and coal yard, November 2004.

Fig. 290   A DMU disappears over the gradient at Gobowen station, towards Shrewsbury, September 2014.

Fig. 291 Croes Newydd North Fork signal box, showing the semaphore home signal for the up goods loop, November 2004.

Fig. 292 Croes Newydd North Fork signal box rear view with signal box-type ventilators on the brick building at the rear, November 2004.

Wrexham was long associated with the coal industry and the last mine at Bersham only closed in 1985. Wrexham is now a centre for light industry and numbers JCB amongst its employers. It is a delightful small town with many buildings of the famous Ruabon brick, as well as the parish church of St Giles, a local landmark.

There was a steel mill at Brymbo, a few miles from Wrexham, until 1990, and limestone was quarried to support the steel mill another few miles beyond that. Steel manufacture generates massive freight traffic on the railways and up until 1982 there was a marshalling yard capable of holding 1,000 wagons at Croes Newydd, a short distance from Wrexham on the way to Brymbo. There were 750 wagons passing through the yard daily in the 1960s.

Leaving the yard towards Wrexham the line split, one branch heading for Chester and the north at North Fork and the other heading south for Shrewsbury at South Fork. There was a signal box at each junction but only North Fork has survived. In the middle of the fork was Croes Newydd engine sheds. Neither of the forks, the yard or anything else survived.

As the line was a hub for coal mining it attracted other railways, and the Wrexham, Mold and Connah's Quay Railway eventually became absorbed by first the Great Central (or rather its predecessor) and then by the LNER. There were three railway stations in Wrexham up until the 1980s: General was the GWR station; Exchange the LNER one that connected to General; and Central, which was the LNER terminus. The remnants of the GWR and LNER survive to this day except that Exchange station was de-named and became part of General. Central still exists in a newer form.

Fig. 291 is a 2004 shot of the box to show a semaphore signal when there were some. The frame has now been removed and there are no longer any mechanical signals here. This box is a survivor though, partly because it controls the junction with the ex-LNER Wrexham–Bidston line. It works absolute block to Penyffordd and there they have a wire-worked distant signal – but that is another story. It also works AB to Gobowen North and TCB to Chester power box. The track, singled in the 1980s, has recently been restored to double to Chester. Unfortunately this undoubted benefit falls short of Wrexham General station, as there is a replacement road underbridge that was put in when the road was improved and that was single track to reflect the track layout at the time. The box

Fig. 293   Croes Newydd North Fork signal box and the up goods loop looking towards the station and Chester, September 2014.

Fig. 294   Croes Newydd North Fork signal box and the station looking towards the box and Shrewsbury, September 2014.

was extended in 1940. Croes Newydd on the name plate should be two separate words.

Looking at Croes Newydd North Fork from the rear (Fig. 292), it looks like the building behind inherited the ventilator cowls from the signal box. This building has now gone. The convenience block is on the back. There are copious amounts of locking frame windows but no frame within.

Fig. 293 is a present-day shot looking north towards Chester. The signal plate numbers appear to have had the date added in as they are in the 900 odds. Perhaps this is part of the grand plan when it goes to an area signalling centre – the CN part of the plate will be dispensed with and the numbers will be all that is required. The up goods loop is on the right but is signalled for trains to leave in the down direction. This signal is the equivalent of the sole semaphore we saw in Fig. 291.

Looking back towards Shrewsbury, we see some of the station track layout in Fig. 294. There are a couple of sidings, one of which is a bay platform, and it was at that platform that the erstwhile Wrexham and Shropshire trains were stabled. The sidings had previously been used for parcels traffic.

Fig. 295   Wrexham General station looking towards Chester, September 2014. The line to the ex-LNER exchange platform is on the left.

Fig. 296   Croes Newydd North Fork signal box crossing keeper's cottage opposite the box, Shrewsbury and Chester Railway, September 2014.

Wrexham General has a fine station building (Fig. 295) similar to the SVR's Kidderminster Town or the long-gone Ross-on-Wye. It is said to be in the French style, at least as far as the roof is concerned. The double tracks head north up the page to Chester, soon to be single and then double as explained in the introductory section to Croes Newydd. The track on the left is an operational platform but is also the connection to the ex-LNER Bidston branch. When Wrexham Exchange was done away with, they built a small platform and extended the footbridge to make contact with what became the new platform four. You can see the extension, which is vaguely in keeping with the GWR original on the left of the picture going out of shot.

The crossing keeper at North Fork crossing originally had a cottage to live in and the building has recently been restored (Fig. 296). It is Shrewsbury and Chester Railway architecture and dates from about 1850 or before. The cottage is across the crossing from the box.

Cornwall

Fig. 297 is a schematic diagram of the boxes plus some of the branches, as this affects the working of the signal boxes concerned. The double tracks are shown with a thicker line than the single lines. The situation with the main line is that although some of the main line was single track at the time of the first survey, the line has been progressively re-doubled since.

Cornwall has been regarded as a Celtic country in its own right with its own language that had some similarities to other Celtic countries. It is a land of great grandeur in its scenery and a beautiful coastline. It also has a rich heritage on the industrial front, with pioneer and innovator Richard Trevithick working in the eighteenth century, mainly with the extensive network of tin mines then in full production. China clay has been exported from Cornwall for centuries and the railways have had a full part to play and still do so. China clay is used in the manufacture of ceramics such as porcelain and glossy magazines, toothpaste and medicines. It is a commonly occurring compound found in most parts of the world.

Where Chester to Wolverhampton was patchy at best in terms of mechanical signalling, Cornwall is the exact opposite. There are five branches, which means a good deal of signalling and junctions that are always fruitful. What was there ten years ago is almost all still there now except for the semaphore distant signals, which have been universally abolished. Fixed distants have been exempt from this cull, at least in the meantime.

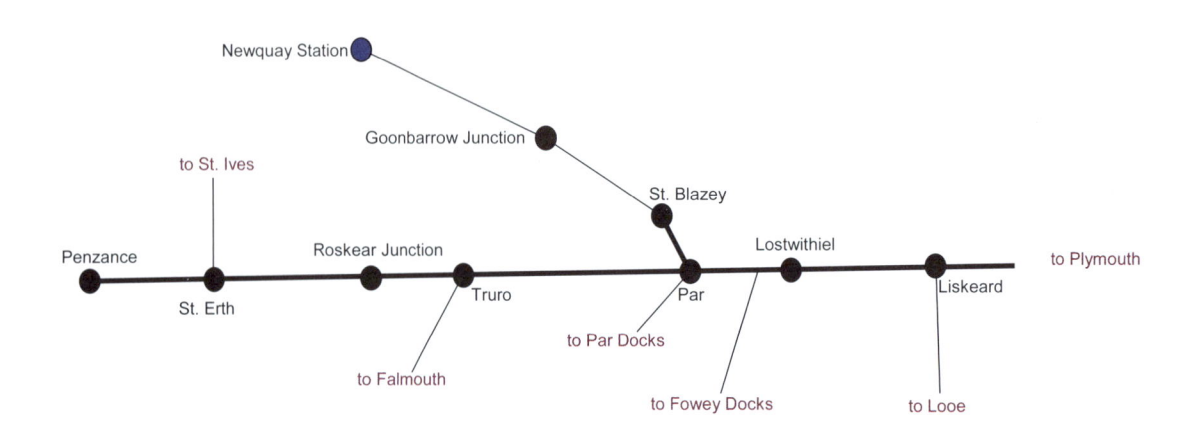

Fig. 297 Diagrammatic representation of the lines in Cornwall and the mechanical signalling there.

Liskeard (LD)

Date Built	1915
GWR Type or Builder	GWR Type 27c
No. of Levers	36
Way of Working	AB, NSKT
Current Status	Active
Listed (Y/N)	N

Liskeard is the first stop on our way west into deeper Cornwall and is an ancient market town that retains an active livestock market. Only 20 miles (32km) from Plymouth, it is also within commuting distance and has a variety of cafés and restaurants.

The station and signal box are a function of the geographical location. The Brunellian station building for the main-line platforms 1 and 2 is way above the platforms, as the platforms sit in a rocky valley. The track is very curvy and undulating in this part of Cornwall and viaducts abound. Set at 90 degrees to platforms 1 and 2 is platform 3, which services the Looe branch line, and this has its own timber station building.

Liskeard signal box, in Fig. 298, is in fine shape for a timber building almost 100 years old. It lacks a cast name plate and ventilators but the sensitive way in which the replacement windows have been done gives the box character. It is internally staircased and there is a yellow walkway for the token exchange for the Looe branch. The box works NSKT, no signaller key token, to Coombe Junction and then OTS from there to Looe. The junction at Coombe is for a freight line to Moorswater, which was the site of a cement works. There is only a ground frame there now. The Liskeard branch platform had its own signal box at one time. The Liskeard box also works AB to Plymouth and Lostwithiel, the next box to the west.

The image in Fig. 299 was taken ten years earlier and is the view towards Lostwithiel. The two home signals expect a train for the west. The photograph was taken from the old footbridge, which has recently been replaced.

The curvature of the line is evident looking towards Plymouth (Fig. 300). The structure just

Fig. 298 Liskeard signal box and the token exchange walkway, September 2014.

Fig. 299 Liskeard station platforms, April 2004. A train is expected for the west and Lostwithiel.

after the trailing crossover is Liskeard viaduct. The point on the left-hand up side is the connection to the Looe branch. This line sees only empty stock passenger trains and freights as there is no facing point lock on the point in the yard at the other end. There is a facing point lock on the point in view, however, as passenger trains to Plymouth have to run over it. The elevated 'ground' disc on the gallows gantry permits entry to the branch.

The gallows gantry signal is shown in more detail in Fig. 301. The photograph was taken from the same level as the main station building and

Fig. 300   Liskeard signal box and the route to Plymouth, September 2014. Note the connection to the Looe branch on the left.

Fig. 301   The up gallows bracket signal detail at Liskeard signal box, September 2014.

Fig. 302   The up gallows bracket signal arm rear detail at Liskeard, September 2014.

car park. Note the pair of red pliers on the platform shelter roof – do they belong to a signal technician?

Fig. 302 is another detail shot of the rear of the centre-balanced home signal on the gallows bracket. The arm is of wood and held together with metal straps. An LED signal lamp is behind the red lens. Note this signal has been modernized with health and safety-conscious ladders and guard rails.

The train from Looe has arrived with a single-car class 150 at platform 3 (Fig. 303). The station building is at 90 degrees to the main running lines, which are behind the camera.

Fig. 303   The Looe branch on platform 3 at Liskeard station, with recent class 150 arrival, April 2004.

Fig. 304   Liskeard viaduct and crossover detail, September 2014.

Fig. 305 Liskeard station on the way to Lostwithiel, September 2014. The up right-hand platform appears to have been extended at some point.

Liskeard viaduct is shown in Fig. 304. There are two sets of rails secured between the running rails on each track. The purpose of these is to detain a derailed vehicle lest it plunge off the viaduct to cause massive damage. Liskeard signal number 4 is a colour light on the up line but a lower quadrant on the down, right-hand side.

Fig. 305, leaving Liskeard for Lostwithiel, emphasizes the switchback nature of the line and its curves. Note also the pull-up boards for trains of up to twelve coaches.

Lostwithiel (LL)

Date Built	1893
GWR Type or Builder	GWR Type 5+
No. of Levers	63
Way of Working	AB, OTS
Current Status	Active
Listed (Y/N)	Y 2013

Lostwithiel is an ancient stannary town dating from the twelfth century, something it shares with Ashburton in Devon. It is known as the antiques capital of Cornwall and it has many cafés and restaurants as well as its own website. A stannary town is one that has to return local taxes to the Duchy of Cornwall.

Lostwithiel signal box has gathered extra duties over the years and it now releases access to the Bodmin and Wenford preserved railway after Bodmin Road signal box closed in 1985. It also controls the access to the Fowey branch, which is worked by OTS. The Fowey branch solely exists for the loading of china clay onto ships by rail. At the end of the branch there is a four-track yard with a loco siding together with discharge equipment for direct loading into the ships. The Fowey branch junction is about half a mile from the box and the box is 277 miles and 34 chains (446.5km) from Paddington. At Lostwithiel there are two groups of sidings as well as up and down goods loops.

Fig. 306 shows a box in fine fettle with a printed name board – saying Lostwithiel Crossing, whereas it appears elsewhere without the 'crossing' qualification. The tunnel under the platform appears to be only for signal wires. The rodding must go elsewhere.

The rear view of the signal box in Fig. 307 is from ten years earlier. Observe the reference to RailTrack on the lock-up box; this outfit ceased to exist after 2002. Also see the adapted window-cleaning apparatus. The chimney stack seems to be the receptacle for a heater flue. The large black cable loom at the rear brings information and indications back to the box.

Fig. 308 shows the Lostwithiel station platforms looking towards the Fowey branch junction and the Penzance direction. At the end of the platforms

Fig. 306 Lostwithiel signal box, September 2014.

Fig. 307 Rear of Lostwithiel signal box, October 2004.

is the start of Lostwithiel viaduct and then straight after that is the Fowey branch junction. Just before the start of the viaduct on the left-hand down side is the point for the four sidings behind the down platform. These used to be used for china clay trains heading to or from the Fowey docks via the branch. These don't seem to see any use now, particularly as the pull-up boards for longer passenger trains appear to be in the yard itself. The nine-car board is on the end of the platform.

Fig. 309 looks the other way, towards Bodmin Parkway and Liskeard. You can see, left to right, the sidings and run-round loop of the Restormel Estates with ground disc exit signal and trap points. The bracket signal smaller arm is for the up goods loop round the corner. Then there is a trailing crossover and, on the far right, the down goods loop.

Fig. 310 returns to 2004, and two trains of china clay wagons await a ship at Fowey docks most likely. The main line is signalled for a train headed for Par and Penzance. It is puzzling what happened to the station buildings here as most others on the line are original or have age to them.

Looking eastbound, the up starter signal has its balance weight halfway up the post (Fig. 311). This is to lessen the chance a passenger being struck with it. In addition the ladder is to the side, as

Fig. 308 Lostwithiel looking westwards to Par, September 2014.

Fig. 309 Lostwithiel looking eastwards and the goods loops, September 2014.

otherwise it would be in the road. The signal on the right is the down goods loop exit signal.

Heading westbound out of Lostwithiel, the next destination of Par is just over 4 miles (6.5km) away. Fig. 312 is again from 2004, as we can see china clay trains stabled on the left, and no jungle in the sidings. Note there are no pull-up boards for trains greater than nine cars at this time.

Lostwithiel signal box is shown in Fig. 313, again in 2004, but looking very little different from the present day.

Par (PR)

Date Built	*c.*1879
GWR Type or Builder	GWR Type 2
No. of Levers	57
Way of Working	AB
Current Status	Active
Listed (Y/N)	N

Fig. 310 Lostwithiel and china clay wagons waiting to go to Fowey docks, October 2004.

Fig. 311 Lostwithiel crossing and starter eastwards, September 2014.

Fig. 312 Lostwithiel china clay storage sidings, October 2004.

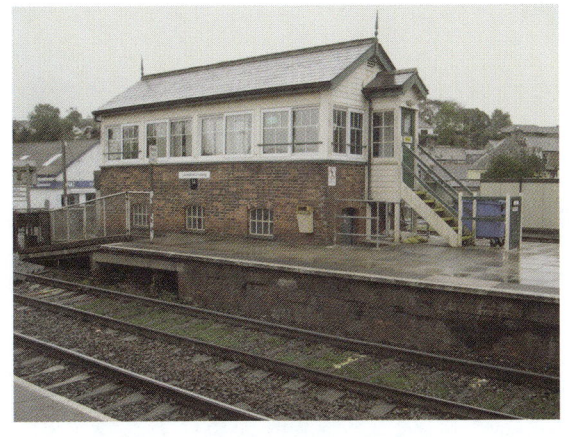

Fig. 313 Lostwithiel signal box, October 2004.

Fig. 314 Par signal box, September 2014.

Par signal box works AB to Lostwithiel and Truro and AB to St Blazey. It is 281 miles and 69 chains (453.6km) from Paddington.

Fig. 314 gives us a glimpse of the outside of Par signal box and an imposing structure it is, if a bit lacking in features such as cowls and cast name plate (although there is a cast name plate on the rear of the box).

Fig. 315 is an overall view of Par station from the eastern end looking towards St Austell and Penzance. The box is at the end of the island platform. The Newquay branch runs in from the right towards the top of the picture and the branch outward home and fixed distant can clearly be seen. The passing loop on the right-hand side appears well used and this is because when the Newquay railcar is stabled in platform 3, china clay trains can still access the branch using the loop. Note the double-railed loop trap point.

There are occasions when all three platforms are occupied by passenger trains.

Moving over to the left at Par in Fig. 316, we can see the trailing crossover and link to enable trains at platform 3 to access the west main line. The refuge siding in front of the box doesn't look well used.

Fig. 317 looks east back to Lostwithiel. The platform starters and the down goods loop exit point are just under the road overbridge on the right. The speed restriction signs mean top is freight and lower DMU passenger. Note the facing crossover beyond the bridge, which is to allow trains from

Par is a small town that gained prosperity in the minerals industry, first through copper and then china clay, which is still a staple of the economic diet. The town has a harbour that was used for china clay shipments but the water is not deep enough to accommodate the larger ocean-going ships, as at Fowey.

Par station is the junction for the Newquay line and before that resort is reached there is a double-track section to St Blazey, a sizeable set of sidings for marshalling china clay trains and a further single-track line to Goonbarrow Junction and thence to Newquay. The station buildings are substantially original and, together with the signal box, give a heritage feel to the place.

Fig. 315 Par station, showing the general layout westwards, September 2014.

Fig. 316 Par station layout westwards to Penzance, September 2014.

the east access to the Newquay branch without reversing.

The Par signal box interior is shown in Fig. 318, with GWR brown lino, polished levers and brasses – the signaller was saying they are polished every Sunday. There are some oddball levers painted blue and white. The points at the east end of the station have been electrified so to switch them over you only need one switch, as the facing point lock movement is integrated electronically. However, because the original facing point lock levers are still part of the mechanical locking in the frame room, the blue and white levers are only moved to complete the facing point interlocking mechanically with other levers, to enable signals to then be selected, for example. The small panel down the bottom is for the re-doubled Burngullow–Probus section.

Fig. 319 shows part of Par signal box track diagram. The 'BH' track circuit is occupied by a train going towards Lostwithiel. The down goods loop is not track circuited and coloured light brown: the significance of the colour is that passenger trains can be held, even though it is not track circuited. To combat any problem this might cause, as the train cannot be seen from the box, the driver is obliged to call the box on the trackside telephone to advise that a train is safely within the loop. We saw something similar at Malvern Wells. At Droitwich Spa there is a tail lamp camera so the signaller can see that the train is safely inside the loop.

The goods loop is fitted with catch points. As you can see, some of the colour light signals are 2 and 3 miles from the box (1 mile = 1,760 yards). The limit of shunt indicator is a device for drivers to move up to but not pass. Usually it is the point at which a shunting train is still visible from the box although this shunt limit is track circuited.

Fig. 320 moves along the signal box diagram. Previously on signal box diagrams there has been a separate number for the facing point lock lever and usually this is the next number in the frame. If you look at the diagram closely you can see that the extra numbers for the facing point locks have been removed using correction fluid. These are the motorized points just referred to, which have

Fig. 317 Par station general layout eastwards, September 2014.

Fig. 318 Par signal box lever frame and block shelf, September 2014.

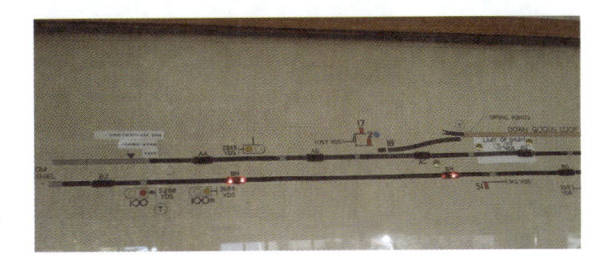

Fig. 319 Par signal box diagram, with train on its way to Lostwithiel, September 2014.

no need of a discrete lever for the facing point lock. Paradoxically, though, the FPL lever is retained to keep the integrity of the mechanical locking. The significance of the 31A and 31B designations on the

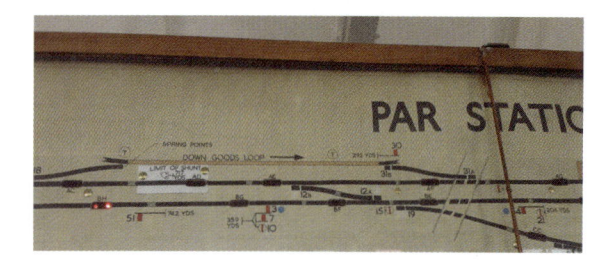

Fig. 320 Par signal box diagram, goods loop and facing point locks, September 2014.

Fig. 321 Par signals P3, P7 and P10, although P10 is hiding in the trees, September 2014.

Fig. 322 Par signal box IBS controller switch, September 2014.

Fig. 323 Par signal box with the track painted white because it can be hot, September 2014.

goods loop is that it is one lever that moves both the point and trap point.

Back outside the box now, Fig. 321 shows the signals opposite the goods loop. Fig. 320 showed a bracket signal with signals 3, 7 and 10 and here they are in reality, although the disc is obscured by the luxuriant growth around it.

Fig. 322 takes a look at the signal box interior, and here is a device we have not met before. The intermediate block section or IBS is used to divide up long block sections so that a train can be in each section, effectively creating another section. It is semi-automatic and uses colour light signals. The reason for it here is the length of time a train may need to get up the incline going towards Lostwithiel. A Voyager needs five minutes, an HST six minutes and a 1,600-tonne china clay train with a class 66 needs eighteen minutes. These eighteen minutes could delay a train coming into the station after a freight train had departed up the incline. Once the freight train is in the IBS it can slog up the bank leaving the section in the station area clear for other movements.

Another oddity we have not met before is the track in Fig. 323, just by Par signal box. It is painted white by the permanent way gang. We have seen the ends of check rails and wing rails painted white before but not this. The signaller explained that as the track at this point has voids beneath it for the point rodding and signal wires coming out of the box, it is seen as a weak spot. High temperatures can cause even modern continuously welded rail to buckle, so the white paint is there to reflect heat and can reduce the surface temperature by 2°C. Note the replacement steel fencing at the back of the platform.

Finally at Par is a class 67 and train that has just come off the Newquay branch with an excursion and is headed for Lostwithiel (Fig. 324). The platform starter that is OFF is for a Wessex Trains

DMU on the adjacent platform, and we can just see a train in the down goods loop beneath the road overbridge.

St Blazey Junction (SB)

Date Built	1908
GWR Type or Builder	GWR Type 7d
No. of Levers	41
Way of Working	AB, KT
Current Status	Active
Listed (Y/N)	N

Now we will take a short excursion up the Newquay branch. St Blazey signal box is exactly half a mile (800m) from Par signal box on a double-track line. This is needed because of the number of china clay trains in the area. The line then goes into single track to Newquay.

There are extensive sidings at St Blazey and a wagon repair shop. Some locomotives are stabled there too and the old steam depot is largely intact. From the yard at St Blazey there is a branch line down to Par Harbour, and although china clay trains still use the branch, the harbour itself is in a state of flux and likely to end up as a marina with housing nearby.

St Blazey signal box also acts as the key token exchange point for the single-track line down the beautiful Luxulyan valley to Goonbarrow Junction. There is another china clay facility at Goonbarrow and the line then is worked OTS to Newquay.

Fig. 325 shows St Blazey signal box looking towards Newquay. Although the windows are sympathetically done, the box has lost some original features though overall it is in good condition. You can just see the old platform ramp of St Blazey station just beyond the box but the station building has been demolished sometime after 1975. The station closed to the public in 1925 but continued to be used mostly for railway workers for the yard and loco depot for years afterwards. The start of the beautiful Luxulyan valley is behind the box. The box works KT to Goonbarrow Junction but there is a permission in that, if a passenger train is

Fig. 324 Par station platform 3 and a class 67 waiting for a DMU on platform 2, October 2004.

on the Goonbarrow to Newquay section, a further token can be removed to enable a china clay train to proceed to Goonbarrow Junction. Otherwise the china clay train would have to wait until the passenger train returned to St Blazey to hand the token back before it could proceed.

Fig. 326 shows St Blazey signal box from the rear. Oddly enough this box does not appear ever to have had coal fires, and now heat is provided by the propane tank. Rear windows give a view of the yard, consisting of a fan of sidings and two mileage sidings. The latter are provided for freight that was

Fig. 325 St Blazey signal box with the former station platform and Luxulyan valley behind, September 2014.

Fig. 326   Rear of St Blazey signal box and propane tank, October 2004.

charged by the mile and carried and unloaded by the customer instead of the railway company. There was not usually any warehouse or goods shed on these sidings.

Fig. 327 shows the double-track main line in front of the box and curving round to the right of the picture. The signal with the home and distant is the equivalent of the signal in Fig. 315 at Par in the top right of that picture, coming back the other way to Par. The siding on the right is for ballast trucks; note the single-railed trap point. The DMU-type railcar is some sort of engineer's vehicle as it is standing in the yard behind the platform.

Following on from the rear view of St Blazey box is Fig. 328. This depicts the fan of sidings to the rear of the box. You can see the various signals going down the branch to Goonbarrow Junction and Newquay, and the manual point levers. There are six sidings in total.

The other side of the yard behind St Blazey box now is shown in Fig. 329. The class 08 locomotive is shunting the yard with an ex-BR brake van that has had air brakes fitted. The wagon repair shops are where the other class 08 is down the yard and the sidings on the extreme left are the washing plant where the china clay wagons get spruced up. Also of note is the red-and-white-striped 'Not to be Moved' sign jokingly attached to the container in the yard on the far right of the picture. The original purpose of these signs was to attach to locomotives that were being worked on in the sheds. This is perhaps a survivor from St Blazey locomotive steam depot.

Looking across the yard now in Fig. 330, you can see the running lines past the front of the box. The device in the middle of the picture – the post, net and hook on the front – is a token catcher apparatus. A train could drop off the token, enclosed in a hoop-like device, onto the hook while the train was in motion. There would be another post where the tablet for the next section was offered to the driver. This meant that a tablet exchange could be performed without needing to stop the train. These

Fig. 327   St Blazey signal box surroundings looking towards Luxulyan station, October 2004.

Fig. 328   Rear of St Blazey signal box and its fan of six sidings, October 2004.

Fig. 329   Rear of St Blazey signal box and the wagon-washing and repair plant, October 2004.

do not appear to have widespread use – the more popular way was to exchange in person with the signaller, either at rest or on the move. This equipment is from the steam age. The ex-BR brake van, then EWS, is of interest as are the horns on the roof, the instanter coupling and air brakes.

Fig. 331 looks at the approaches to St Blazey from Par, and on the left is the exit signal, SB41, from the Par docks branch. The class 08 with tanker wagons with what looks like heavy oil is heading for the locomotive depot perhaps. The ballast wagon siding is to the right.

On the Par docks branch, another steam-age heritage item is shown in Fig. 332. The wooden level-crossing gates are passing into history and these are train crew operated. These were being painted at the time so would seem to have a future. The view is looking towards the china clay dries, where the product is transformed into a powder-like substance.

Fig. 330   St Blazey signal box and steam-age token catcher, October 2004.

Fig. 331   St Blazey class 08 shunts oil tankers for depot, October 2004.

Fig. 332   St Blazey–Par harbour branch and wooden crossing gates, September 2014.

Fig. 333   St Blazey steam-age roundhouse, October 2004.

The former St Blazey steam locomotive depot is shown in Fig. 333 and is of the roundhouse variety but, unusually in Britain, the turntable is in the open. The roundhouse sheds are being put to other light industrial uses now.

Goonbarrow Junction (G)

Date Built	*c.*1909
GWR Type or Builder	GWR Type 7d
No. of Levers	25
Way of Working	KT, OTS
Current Status	Active
Listed (Y/N)	N

Heading up the Luxulyan valley from St Blazey towards Newquay, you come to the somewhat isolated Goonbarrow Junction signal box. It was the junction for the lines to Carbis (not to be confused with Carbis Bay on the St Ives branch) and Gunheath, both of which were closed many years ago. It is still a junction with the Newquay branch and Imerys Pigments china clay dries site. The box works KT with St Blazey and OTS from the junction to Newquay.

The signal box itself exists in a seeming time warp and looks almost completely original, except for the windows and lack of ventilators. The drying sheds for Imerys Pigments are behind the box.

Fig. 334   Goonbarrow Junction signal box, October 2004.

Fig. 335   Goonbarrow Junction signal box from the rear with matching coal bunker, October 2004.

Fig. 336 Goonbarrow Junction signal box, looking towards St Blazey, October 2004.

Fig. 337 Goonbarrow Junction, October 2004. A class 150 heads for Newquay, with china clay sidings on the left.

Goonbarrow Junction from the rear, in Fig. 335, boasts the attractive rounded engineer's blue brick to finish it all off and this even extends to the coal bunker on the left, although, as at St Blazey, there is no evidence of a fireplace. The conclusion must be that these boxes had pot-bellied stoves instead.

Behind the box are three sidings for the china clay wagons but originally belonging to EWS. Note there is bullhead rail in the foreground supported on GWR two-bolt fixing chairs; other railways used three bolts.

Looking back along the line towards Luxulyan station and St Blazey (Fig. 336), the running lines past the box consist of a passing loop with an up refuge siding. The bracket signal at the end of the box controls the line to Newquay and the entry point to the china clay sidings. The token exchange walkway extends across both tracks; the left-hand track is up towards Paddington and the right-hand down to Newquay. The box is 287 miles and 40 chains (462.7km) from Paddington, and 15 miles and 9 chains (24.3km) from Newquay station.

The view of the entry point to the china clay complex in Fig. 337 is from the rear of the box. On the far left are china clay wagons awaiting loading. Towards the centre, next track along, is the entry to a run-round loop where locomotives are uncoupled

Fig. 338 Goonbarrow Junction signal box diagram, October 2004.

and run round the train. Finally, on the right by the concrete hut, a class 150 makes its way to Newquay.

Inside Goonbarrow Junction box now, Fig. 338 shows the track layout diagram. The passing loop in front of the box is in black so is track circuited. It has been modified on the St Blazey end and this may have been to do with the signalling. Note that the distant signal on the end is a fixed distant and this is commonplace on branch lines that have a moderate line speed. The bracket signal referred to in Fig. 336 consists of signals 24, 20 and 23.

Fig. 339 Goonbarrow Junction signal box lever frame, with only one spare, October 2004.

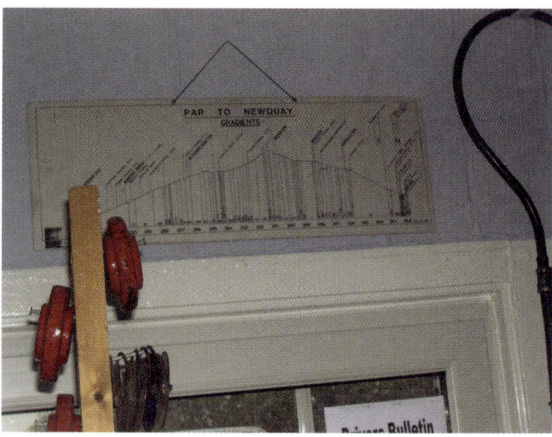

Fig. 340 The Par–Newquay gradient profile at Goonbarrow Junction and the tablet hoop on the right, October 2004.

Each of the four points that form the double crossover of the passing loop has an associated facing point lock (FPL) lever with an 'a' designation. The up refuge siding at the top of the diagram is considered to be a trailing point only and so has no FPL. The siding off the passing loop towards Newquay is known as the 'Bugle siding' as Bugle is the next station in the Newquay direction.

Fig. 339 is the signal box lever frame and looks well looked after. There is only one white lever, indicating that the layout here has not changed much since the frame was installed in 1925. The key token apparatus, the red box at the end, is at the St Blazey end of the box as per normal practice. The ivorine plates on the signal levers indicate not only what that lever does but the order in which other levers must be pulled that interlock with that lever. Note there are no yellow levers, as all distant signals on the branch are fixed.

Fig. 340 shows a gradient profile of the Newquay branch. These were especially useful in the days when runaway vehicles were a real possibility if not manually braked properly. The signaller could see from the diagram where a runaway was likely to go and then take action to divert it away from the running lines if possible. There have been several incidents in the past where runaway wagons have created mayhem. All vehicles must now have brakes that automatically come on when the vehicle is uncoupled from a locomotive and so the need for the gradient diagram is not so pressing. The diagrams still help with line management, however, for example when a signaller may wish to put a slower train in a loop or refuge.

The numbers at the bottom of the diagram are miles from Paddington. The hoop-type device on the right is the holder for the key token, which could either be exchanged manually or by apparatus as described under St Blazey (*see* Fig. 330). Note the lever collars that are stacked up together with warning signs not to pull a certain lever as that element is being worked on.

Signal 24, as we saw from Fig. 338, gives the all clear to a train for Newquay, given that all token procedures have been completed (Fig. 341).

Truro (T)

Date Built	1899
GWR Type or Builder	GWR Type 7a
No. of Levers	54
Way of Working	AB, OTS
Current Status	Active
Listed (Y/N)	N

Fig. 341 The Goonbarrow Junction bracket signal expects a train to Newquay, the two elevated discs are for the china clay sidings of Imerys Pigments, October 2004.

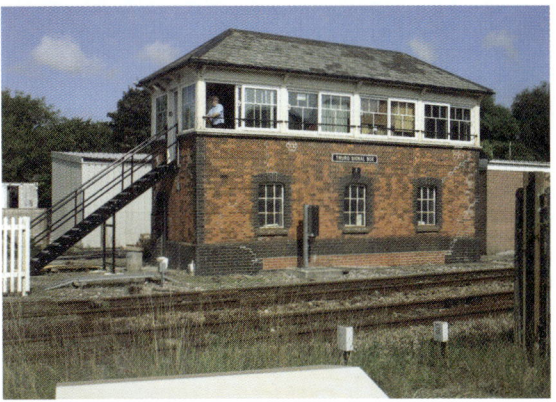

Fig. 342 Truro signal box with the barriers coming down, September 2014.

Fig. 343 Rear of Truro signal box with wooden staircase, October 2004.

The only city in Cornwall and its chief administrative centre, Truro is our next stop. The cathedral is a comparatively recent acquisition in 1910 but Truro has many fine Georgian buildings and was a stannary town for the mining industry. The railway is the junction for the port of Falmouth, to which it works OTS. Falmouth is renowned as a deep-water port and it is not unusual to see ocean-going ships moored in the estuary of the River Fal. Truro was also the junction for another branch line to Newquay via Chacewater but this closed many years ago. There was also a large motive power depot here in steam days.

The signal box at Truro is another piece of preserved work although it looks as though the brickwork has been cracking. The tunnel for rodding and signal wires from the frame room was bricked up some years ago, although there is another at the rear of the box. Fig. 342 also shows the signaller at a crossing control panel, as a road runs right by the box and divides the station from the signal box area.

The rear and side of the signal box are shown in Fig. 343; this is a retro photograph, as the box still has its replacement wooden staircase in this view. Note the tunnel for signal wires and rodding at the rear and that the doors appear to be in Western Region brown.

The ramp at platform 2 at Truro station shows the line curving away eastwards to St Austell and

Fig. 344   Truro signal box and the way to Par, September 2014.

Fig. 345   Truro station looking westwards, September 2014. The Falmouth train is leaving.

Par (Fig. 344). The sighting board on signal T6 seems a bit odd but we're not looking at it from a driver's point of view.

The west end of Truro station, towards Penzance, provides the view in Fig. 345. On the left, the Falmouth train, class 150, is leaving from platform 1 past its starter signal. Note that the trap point is closed. The sidings on the far side used to be for EWS but appear disused now. The industrial building on the left in the distance and beyond is where the steam locomotive depot used to be. It was the cost of hauling locomotive coal this far west that prompted the GWR to consider electrification in the 1940s.

Fig. 346 shows a class 150 waiting at platform 3 heading a local train to Newton Abbot in Devon. The architecture here has similarities to Stourbridge Junction and Wrexham General. Note there is a banner repeater signal for signal T47, which we saw on the end of platform 2 in Fig. 345.

The passenger entrance at Truro station (Fig. 347) shows similarities to Kidderminster Town, on the Severn Valley Railway, and Wrexham General. There is a 1960s/70s piece tacked, carbuncle like, on at the end. Truro station is 300 miles and 63 chains (484.1km) from Paddington.

Roskear Junction (R)

Date Built	c.1895
GWR Type or Builder	GWR Type 5
No. of Levers	Nil
Way of Working	AB
Current Status	Active
Listed (Y/N)	N

Fig. 346   A class 150 for Newton Abbot is waiting at Truro station, September 2014. Note the banner repeater for the signal on the end of the platform in Fig. 345.

Fig. 347   Truro station building in the style of others, September 2014.

Roskear Junction signal box is 16 chains from Camborne station but was retained as it had a junction to Roskear Goods up until 1983 as well as being a crossing place.

Camborne was famous as the centre of the Cornish tin mining industry and even had its own school of mining. It has a population about the size of Truro. Richard Trevithick, who came from nearby, invented and ran the first steam locomotive to power itself on the roads in 1801. There were many other inventions attributed to him mainly to do with mining. He is commemorated in Camborne with a statue and remembered every year.

Roskear Junction signal box is that unusual beast in Cornwall in that it is a haven of colour light signals and yet uses AB signalling equipment. It does not have a frame, only an individual function switch (IFS) panel.

Fig. 348 shows that Roskear Junction is like Bentley Heath Crossing in the sense that there is a handily placed footbridge to enable members of the public to cross the railway when the barriers are down. The only variation to the double-track layout here is a trailing crossover. The signal box would appear to be a target for antisocial behaviour like Sutton Bridge Junction judging by the wire mesh grilles on all windows.

Roskear Junction signal box interior and signal box diagram are shown in Fig. 349. The station at Camborne has a train ready to start plunger, which is a message to the signaller, who has a similar device in the box. We can see that the Roskear Goods section has been edited out with correction fluid and there is also reference to the 29-lever frame that is no longer there. The sole points on the diagram are clipped and padlocked, meaning that trains will not be doing any crossover work here. The diagram also says 'Bolted normal' for points lever 15. Roskear Junction also controls the barrier crossing at Camborne station.

Roskear Junction signal box block shelf (Fig. 350) boasts a GWR 1947 block instrument and block bell for the next westwards block post at St Erth. In between is a Welwyn control release. On the left are two plungers, both black Bakelite with a brass knob

Fig. 348 Roskear Junction signal box, October 2004.

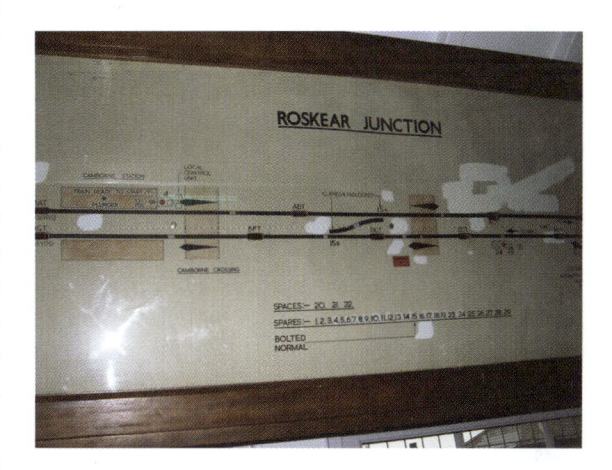

Fig. 349 Roskear Junction signal box diagram, October 2004.

Fig. 350 Roskear Junction signal box block shelf with St Erth instruments, October 2004.

153

Fig. 351 Roskear Junction signal box IFS units and CCTV monitor, October 2004.

Fig. 352 Camborne station in the Edwardian style, October 2004.

on, and they are the bell plungers for Camborne and Redruth stations, the equivalent of what is on the platforms. The CCTV monitor is for a crossing.

The signal box block shelf has two IFS units (Fig. 351), one controlling the barriers and the other a signal. Signal R4 is the colour light on the up platform at Camborne station.

Camborne station (Fig. 352) has a GWR Edwardian station building, which is not unlike Henley-in-Arden in style though it is not as big and with no canopies or shelter. Signal R4 referred to in Fig. 351 is just to the right of the picture.

St Erth (SE)

Date Built	1899
GWR Type or Builder	GWR Type 5
No. of Levers	69
Way of Working	AB
Current Status	Active
Listed (Y/N)	N

St Erth is the junction for the St Ives branch and is a village steeped in history, with early records of a saint who spread Christianity to the area. The Hayle river provided an obstacle to trade until a causeway was built in the early nineteenth century. St Ives has now become an extremely popular tourist destination again after the founding of the Tate St Ives gallery, dedicated to modern art. Many artists found inspiration at St Ives in the 1930s and this movement has regained momentum in recent years.

St Erth station and signal box have survived surprisingly well over the years and, goods facilities apart, little has changed since the steam era. St Erth signal box is 320 miles and 63 chains (516.3km) from Paddington.

Fig. 353 St Erth signal box looking eastwards, September 2014.

Fig. 354   St Erth signal box rear with wooden staircase, October 2004.

Fig. 355   St Erth looking westwards, September 2014.

Fig. 356   A class 150 arrives at St Erth on its way to Penzance, September 2014.

The signal box in Fig. 353 is unusual that it has been painted in the old GWR structure colours of light stone and dark stone, harking back to the 1930s. The hanging basket is a recent domestication but the lucky horseshoe has been there a while. Note that there is a pull-up board for a twelve-coach train just by the box.

The rear of St Erth in earlier days is illustrated in Fig. 354. Note the masses of point rodding and signal wires that are coming out of the back of the box. The St Ives branch runs in at the back of the box so there is an additional name plate there. Also of note is the wooden staircase.

Fig. 355 is the view looking towards Penzance from the footbridge. Worthy of note is the fact that the line is equipped for running in both directions towards Penzance.

Fig. 356 shows the St Erth station layout. The main line from Camborne and Truro runs in at the top of the picture, and the class 150 is bound for Penzance, which is only a little under 5 miles (8km) away by rail. The St Ives branch comes into the bay platform just behind the bracket signal and the connection to the main running line. We have been used to seeing bracket signals with a subsidiary goods arm but this time the connection is for passenger trains, and, like the bracket signal at Par, by the box for the Newquay line, the arms are the same size. The loading bay siding next to the bay starter signal is behind the bracket signal. The two platform shelters nearest the viewer are later additions, when holiday crowds would disgorge from holiday trains and then make their way to St Ives via the branch. The St Ives portion of the Cornish Riviera Express was massively expanded to eleven coaches or so and run down the branch in one piece. The stone waiting room by the DMU is part of the original accommodation.

Some detail of the arrangements of rodding and signal wires appears in Fig. 357. The scene is behind

155

Fig. 357   St Erth behind the signal box, detail of wires and point rodding, October 2004.

the box with the St Ives branch to the left, and the point in the picture leads either to the bay platform 3 or the loading bay at platform 4. The rodding is to operate the point and a facing point lock. The two signal wires are for home signals, one in each direction. The junction between platforms 3 and 4 and the main line are signalled by a colour light with a modern version of an elevated ground disc, the post and ladder of which are just in the shot at the top of the picture. There had been a semaphore bracket signal, and just a bit further down the branch were sidings for United Dairies. The guard rails from bullhead rail are another notable feature.

Fig. 358 looks towards the east and Camborne. The GWR platform seats at figure 358 are of two types. One has cast ends with timbers holding the ends together, and the other is an all-wood bench, not normally found without a shelter. The wooden panelling of the platform shelter is typical of GWR wayside structures (there is a splendidly preserved example at Bewdley on the Severn Valley Railway). To the right, by the ground disc, is the lead-off to two goods sidings, which don't seem to see any use now. Platform 4 on the extreme left is just a loading dock as it doesn't extend even this far.

Fig. 359 focuses on the buffer stops on the St Ives bay at St Erth and a delightful stone station building. Only bullhead rail is found here, and that includes the buffer stops, which have different crosspieces of rail and wood. The rail type appears to have had a bump at some point. In past years there would have been a signal lamp placed on top of the crosspieces to warn drivers but now there is the high-intensity red lighting in a driver's line of vision, which is probably safer although aesthetically less pleasing.

Fig. 358 (left centre)   St Erth looking eastwards on platform 2 with period shelter and seats, October 2004.

Fig. 359   St Erth, St Ives bay and loading bay, platforms 3 and 4, October 2004.

Fig. 360　St Erth, period shelters and original footbridge looking towards Penzance, October 2004.

Fig. 361　St Erth looking towards St Ives, October 2004.

The view in Fig. 360 is looking towards Penzance. The two shelters referred to in Fig. 356 are in view, as is the trailing crossover beyond the platforms and the line of pull-up boards for longer passenger trains. In the case of a longer train, the signaller must pull off SE6 on the down platform on the left to admit the train to pull up beyond the end of the platform.

Finally, Fig. 361 shows the two passenger platforms; platform 3, which is the bay for St Ives; and platform 4, which is no more than a loading dock. The oily sleepers on the platform 3 track are clear evidence of where the St Ives DMU pulls up. This view is from ten years ago and the station car park is now crammed to capacity, indicative of the increase in rail travel in recent years. This is reflected in the fact that the station now sees sixty-nine trains per average day and these are almost equally divided between down and up and the St Ives branch. It is the busiest service station in Cornwall and one of the busiest rural stations in the country.

Penzance (PZ)

Date Built	1938
GWR Type or Builder	GWR Type 12b
No. of Levers	75
Way of Working	AB
Current Status	Active
Listed (Y/N)	N

Penzance has long been an administrative centre and a connecting point to the Isles of Scilly. Ships used to ply this route and now it is helicopters. Penzance saw a huge trade in boxes of cut flowers from the Scilly Islands, most of which went to London Covent Garden market by rail. In 1938 alone there were 4,891 *tonnes* of cut flowers forwarded by the GWR.

In addition, the broccoli trade used to see literally trainfuls of the vegetable loaded at Long Rock sidings, just along from Penzance station. From Cornwall as a whole – and Penzance featured largely in this – there were 450 special trains

Fig. 362　Penzance signal box, October 2004.

Fig. 363 Penzance signal box, window and frame detail, October 2004.

consisting of 20,240 wagonloads of broccoli dispatched in 1938.

Penzance is at the end of the line and almost the end of Britain. While the sea has been promised here and there through Cornwall, at Penzance it is a reality. Consequently the track layout here is very linear, as the sea wall forms one boundary.

Penzance signal box, in Fig. 362, is a bit of a hybrid, with a full 75-lever frame but not actually operating any wire-operated signals or rodded points. All equipment is electrically operated and the signal levers just operate switches. However, there is a mechanical interlocking frame, which still works. The signal levers that are not spares, or white painted, are physically smaller than usual so as to remind signallers not to use excessive force, as it is not needed. The box looks as though it had ventilators at one point but perhaps they are now in the Atlantic Ocean. Original windows were still there in 2004. The only signalling equipment coming out of this box is a cable duct and its contents.

Fig. 363 gives a closer view. You can see the smaller levers in the frame compared with the white spares. There is only one set of block instruments, and you can see the block bell on the shelf. Although the box is less than seventy years old at this point it is displaying the ravages inflicted by the weather.

Penzance station is a celebration in Cornish granite and looks quite sprightly, considering it was opened in 1879 (Fig. 364). Platforms 1, 2 and 3 are within the overall roof of the train shed and platform 4 is the one facing the reader. There is still an end loading dock with a ramp up to it so that vehicles can be driven onto trains. Next to that, and nearest of all to the reader, is a parcels siding. In the essentially pre-motorway days British Railways operated a service known as Motorail, where passengers embarked their cars on special coaches and then rode in ordinary passenger coaches attached to the same train. The attraction was that the car

Fig. 364 Penzance station general view, October 2004.

Fig. 365 Penzance station platform 4 and welcome rock, October 2004.

Fig. 366 Penzance Long Rock with former goods loading on the left and TMD in the distance, October 2004.

Fig. 367 HST leaving Penzance station bound for Paddington on the single line, October 2004.

driver was saved the incredibly long and tedious journey with the obligatory several-hour wait at the 'Exeter Bypass', particularly if this journey was undertaken on a bank holiday.

Fig. 365 shows the station and end of platform 4. The delightful stone station building is blessed with towering chimney stacks. Note the colour light signals and the box apparently beneath the right-hand one. The welcome message on the rock is in Cornish as well as English. The buffer stops at Penzance station are 326 miles and 50 chains (525.7km) from Paddington.

Moving on to Long Rock now along from the box and station (Fig. 366), the view is towards St Erth. The area to the left was the goods yard and the broccoli trains mentioned in the Penzance introduction used to be loaded here. Note that there are oil tanker wagons for refuelling the HSTs, Voyagers and other DMUs serviced at the traction maintenance depot in the distance. The tracks here are: the up and down main line (on the right); then what had originally been a carriage reception road but now provides access to Long Rock HST depot; and a loop line on the left.

An HST heads up towards Paddington from Penzance station and is about to head off to Marazion, where it will pass St Michael's Mount on the right and St Erth (Fig. 367). The depot access road and loop are now on the right-hand side of the picture.

The Absorbed Lines

These lines are former separate companies, smaller than the GWR, which lost their identity in the grouping of all railways in 1923. Most of the lines absorbed were Welsh and all of the survivors are Welsh. I have not considered the absorbed narrow gauge lines in the survey.

Cambrian Railways

The line ran from Oswestry, where the headquarters was, and Whitchurch in Shropshire through mid-Wales to the Cardigan Bay coast. The line then split into two and went north to Pwllheli and south to Aberystwyth. Most of the line survives except that the Oswestry and Whitchurch connections are lost. The line connects with the rest of the system at Sutton Bridge Junction Shrewsbury, which we have already visited. The Cambrian headquarters at Oswestry survives and there is preservation activity there.

In Fig. 368 there are no block post signal boxes in the accepted sense apart from Machynlleth. The Cambrian lines were converted to RETB in the 1980s with Machynlleth as its hub and more recently to ERTMS as a trial with a view to adopting this system for the rest of the network. Consequently none of the former absolute block system survives and it is remarkable that any semaphore signalling or its infrastructure remains.

159

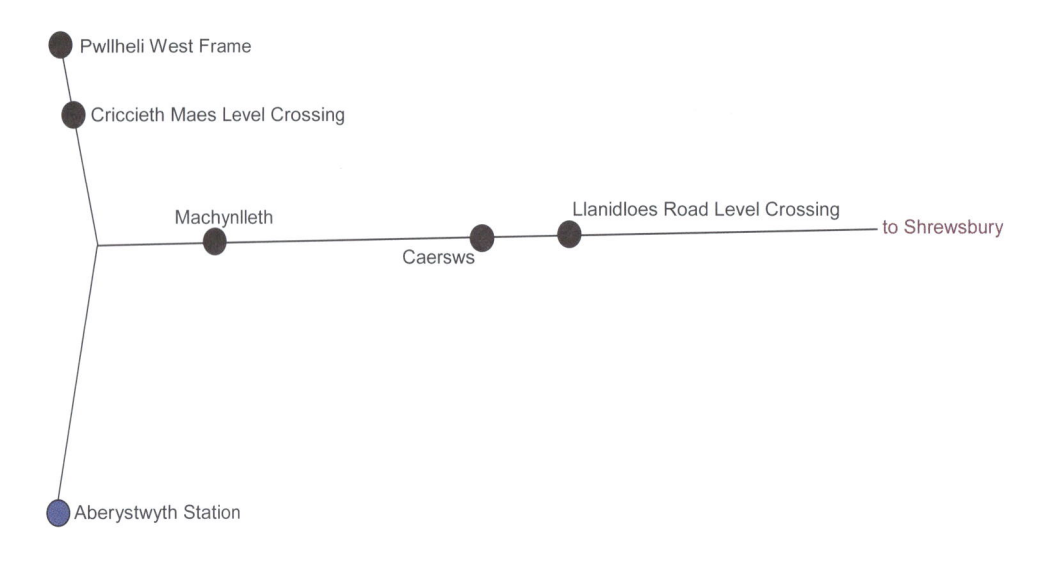

Fig. 368 Cambrian Railways mechanical signalling disposition.

Llanidloes Road Level Crossing

The line begins its journey through mid-Wales through Welshpool and Newtown, and just west of Newtown is the crossing. It had a ground frame and three signal levers and manually operated gates, as shown in Fig. 369. The diagram is pinned to the wooden board in front of the three home signal levers.

Fig. 370 shows a home and fixed distant for Llanidloes Road. The scenery in mid-Wales is

Fig. 369 Llanidloes Road level crossing lever frame and gate, September 2009.

Fig. 370 Llanidloes Road level crossing home and distant signals, September 2009.

Caersws (CS)

Date Built	1891
GWR Type or Builder	Dutton (Cambrian)
No. of Levers	18
Way of Working	Gate box
Current Status	Inactive
Listed (Y/N)	Y

Caersws was the junction for the Van branch line, and the box (Fig. 371) was retained in use until March 2011. Caersws station is an award winner for unstaffed stations, with Cambrian stone architecture and decoration.

Fig. 372 looks eastwards towards Newtown. Note the stone-built goods shed on the right of the line and, if you peer carefully, the bracket semaphore home signal guarding the crossing. Caersws is 53 miles and 31 chains (85.9km) from Sutton Bridge Junction Shrewsbury.

Machynlleth (MH)

Date Built	1960
GWR Type or Builder	BR WR 37e+
No. of Levers	50
Way of Working	RETB
Current Status	Demolished 2011
Listed (Y/N)	N

Machynlleth is a pretty market town nestling in the hills of mid-Wales. The station is the feeder point for Dovey Junction, where the line splits to go north and south along the coast. It is also the control point for the ERTMS signalling system that came into use in March 2011. This system control room occupies a new building opposite the site of the signal box

Fig. 373   Machynlleth signal box and the old steam shed in use as a DMU depot, September 2008.

Fig. 371   Caersws signal box, September 2008.

Fig. 372   Caersws signal box, gates and disused goods shed, with the home signal down the line, September 2008.

Fig. 374   Machynlleth station, September 2008. Note the staggered platforms.

depicted, which has been demolished. The box was 75 miles and 4 chains (120.8km) from Sutton Bridge Junction.

Before demolition the box controlled not only the Cambrian system with RETB but the local station and yard. Fig. 373 depicts the box in operation, looking back towards Caersws. There are upper and lower quadrant signals and an 1863-built locomotive depot still in use for the purpose for which it was built. A class 158 is inside the depot.

Fig. 374 clearly shows the staggered platform layout at Machynlleth and the scale of the station building on the down left-hand side. The up side has a wooden shelter. The view is looking towards Dovey Junction, 4 miles (6.5km) away.

Maes Level Crossing, Criccieth

Criccieth is a particularly attractive small town and seaside resort with an imposing castle overlooking the beach. It has a fine hotel and some choice restaurants. It has an interesting history with some famous people associated with it.

A short way from the station was a gated crossing attended by a keeper, who was provided with a pretty cottage with a view of the sea and castle. The crossing and keeper were replaced by barriers in 2009.

Fig. 375 is the crossing keeper's cottage and ground frame. Brown levers are to lock the gates and the red are for signals. The keeper was provided with the Portakabin structure. Previously all railway-related equipment that was indoors was inside the cottage. At other places a block instrument showing the state of the block would be in the sitting room, to give good warning that a train was coming.

Pwllheli West Frame

Date Built	1909
GWR Type or Builder	Dutton Type 2 (Cambrian)
No. of Levers	4
Way of Working	Shunt frame
Current Status	Active
Listed (Y/N)	N

Fig. 375   Criccieth ground frame and home signal, February 2009.

Pwllheli is primarily a seaside resort that was popularized in the 1930s by Billy Butlin's Holiday Camp, and in those days most people went by rail. This same effect was seen at Minehead, Ayr, Skegness, Clacton and Filey, where a special station was built just for the holiday camp trains. Pwllheli now has a smart new marina.

The West Frame box is a box without signals just as Maes Crossing was signals without a box. It is used to operate points at the station for the down siding and headshunt. There is another frame for the loop.

Fig. 377 shows the fairly cavernous interior of Pwllheli station, where throngs of holidaymakers in the 1950s would be passing through to Butlin's.

Barry Railway

The Barry Railway, as many others in South Wales, was constructed primarily to move coal; in particular, it moved coal for export from Cardiff docks. The Barry Railway was very successful and made its promoters and backers rich, as the distances from pit to port were small and the infrastructure needed was moderate. The port of Barry is still prominent in the movement of chemicals, minerals, steel and scrap and dry bulk materials.

It was here near the signal box that Dai Woodham had nearly 300 steam locomotives stored ready for scrapping in the 1960s, 1970s and 1980s. He was too busy to attend to the locos as he had a contract to cut up 1,000 steel mineral wagons and they were easier to do than locomotives. As a result, many steam locomotives were saved and preserved, and are running today.

Fig. 376 Pwllheli West Frame ground frame, July 2006.

Fig. 377 Pwllheli station and the Butlin's concourse, July 2006.

Fig. 378 Barry signal box, September 2006.

Barry (B)

Date Built	*c.*1897
GWR Type or Builder	Barry Type 1
No. of Levers	77
Way of Working	–
Current Status	Closed
Listed (Y/N)	N

Fig. 379   Barry station and docks branch, September 2006.

Barry signal box (Fig. 378) is a product of the signalling company Evans O'Donnell and is said to be a copy of a design originally used on the Great Eastern Railway. There is a connection to Barry Docks behind the box and that is also where the former Barry locomotive depot stood until a few years ago at least. It was also where Dai Woodham had his scrapyard.

Fig. 379 shows Barry station looking towards Bridgend and Swansea. The docks and former engine shed are to the left of the line that curves left down to Barry Island, which is a popular holiday resort and still rail served. The line between the Barry Island branch and the main line is the down goods loop.

Aberthaw (AW)

Date Built	1897
GWR Type or Builder	Barry Type 2
No. of Levers	53
Way of Working	AB, TCB
Current Status	Closed
Listed (Y/N)	Y

Aberthaw signal box stands on the disused platform of a former station but its duties in later years were mainly freight related, serving Aberthaw cement works and the coal-fired power station of the same name.

Fig. 380 shows the box on the platform seemingly sinking from a blizzard of paperwork in the windows. Perhaps it can be very sunny and the paperwork is a defence. The platform looks as though it is covered with modelling brick paper that has not been matched up properly. The box's future is now uncertain as it is rather isolated for anyone to care for it. Perhaps the best solution is donation to a preserved railway in Wales.

Fig. 381 is a view towards Barry station and junction. In front of the box are the main running lines, and then next to the platform is the down passing loop with sidings off to the left; a lone merry-go-round wagon occupies one of the sidings.

Beyond that are the former EWS reception sidings for the power station, then past the rear of

Fig. 380   Aberthaw signal box, September 2006.

164

the box is a further loop line to allow the main line to be regained on the west side.

London and the Home Counties

A liberty has been taken by including Oxfordshire as a home county when the general view is that it is not. A plea in mitigation is offered in that Oxfordshire did not have anywhere else to go. In the southeast of England GWR mechanical signalling or former mechanical signal boxes on Network Rail are sparse indeed.

The boxes considered are:

Banbury North, Oxfordshire
Banbury South, Oxfordshire
Colthrop Crossing, Berkshire
Greenford East Junction, London Borough of Ealing

None of them, except Banbury, have any connection to each other and so a route diagram is not practicable.

Banbury North (BN)

Date Built	1900
GWR Type or Builder	GWR Type 7b
No. of Levers	95
Way of Working	TCB, AB
Current Status	Active
Listed (Y/N)	N

Banbury is a market town in north Oxfordshire and within commuting range of London and Birmingham. It is also a considerable administrative and commercial centre for the predominantly rural surrounding, and is famous for Banbury cakes.

The station and signal boxes lie on the route from London to Birmingham Snow Hill, and Banbury had the distinction of the last GWR slip coach operation in 1960. A slip coach was a means of uncoupling a coach from a train at speed and bringing the coach into a station on its own, or to a stand by a special guard on the coach. The original station of 1850 was a timber building; it was replaced in 1958, some say before it fell down. It was due to be replaced by the art deco type of station that Leamington Spa had received before World War II. The signal boxes escaped largely unscathed and semaphore signals were retained on the rebuild.

There was a connection to the LNER here and the milk trains from Dorrington in Shropshire (*see* the introduction to Dorrington in the Shrewsbury–Hereford section), changed engines here. Banbury also had a marshalling yard to deal with the Oxfordshire ironstone traffic, which was appreciable.

Fig. 381 Aberthaw general layout and power station sidings, September 2006.

Fig. 382 Banbury North signal box, November 2004.

Fig. 383   Banbury North signal box rear view and traffic, November 2004.

The way of working to Leamington Spa in the north is TCB, while its near neighbour of Banbury South is worked to by AB. Banbury North is the second largest remaining ex-GWR signal box in terms of levers still in active use.

The rear of the box is shown in Fig. 383. There's quite a bit of operational interest here, with a Chiltern Trains DMU that has been put into the down goods loop. The small siding signal has been replaced behind the train but the point into the loop has yet to be replaced back to normal. This is just the way the interlocking works. Banbury North is unusual in that the lever frame levers face the rear of the box when normal rather than the windows.

The class 47/57 and container train is halted at the up goods loop exit upper quadrant semaphore signal and from here a freight train is routed round the back of the station platforms. The line on the far right is termed the up goods siding. The other two tracks between the two diesels are the main running lines. The down goods loop is a long one and the facing crossover on the right-hand down main line is to allow a second train into the loop if the first part is occupied.

Fig. 382 shows a signal box in fine fettle, with extremely well done replacement windows and wooden staircase. Cowl ventilators and an original cast name plate are also present and enhance the period look.

The area has been part of the London Midland Region and its successors since the 1960s so it is no surprise to see an upper quadrant signal peering out from behind the box. As at Shrewsbury, there are upper and lower quadrant semaphores and colour light signals.

Fig. 384 is a general view of Banbury North, with the up siding starter home signal with fixed distant beneath on the right. Moving across is the up goods loop starter and fixed distant beneath. The colour light signal next to that is for the up main line.

Fig. 384   Banbury North general layout and goods sidings, November 2004.

Fig. 385   Banbury station looking north, November 2004.

Fig. 386 Banbury station and the three northbound signals, September 2014.

Fig. 385 looks north towards Leamington Spa. Despite the station building's pseudo-modernity, there are lower quadrant semaphore signals at the two platform ends.

Fig. 386 is the down end of Banbury station, looking towards Leamington Spa. The bracket signal, BN4, is for the down relief road, and will be used for a freight train shortly, and the lower quadrant home to the right of the bracket is the bay platform home signal. The colour light signal is the down main platform starter. Banbury North box is just beyond the overbridge.

Fig. 387 shows the up goods roads with the two former cattle sidings converted into DMU servicing roads. This work was done in connection with the Reading station rebuilding work to accommodate First Great Western and Chiltern Trains. Note that the track is all bullhead rail until it comes to the two sidings on the right, which have been relaid in the more modern flat-bottomed rail. Note that the bay platform on the left is where the DMUs have been parked, judging by the oil on the track bed.

Banbury South (BS)

Date Built	1908
GWR Type or Builder	GWR Type 7d
No. of Levers	67
Way of Working	AB, TCB
Current Status	Active
Listed (Y/N)	N

Fig. 387 Banbury station and the former cattle sidings, September 2014.

Fig. 388 Banbury South signal box, September 2014.

Fig. 389 Banbury South signal box rear view, September 2014.

Banbury South is as well preserved as North, with excellent reproduction windows. It has had its frame size reduced in recent years to accommodate a panel and VDU to control parts of the line to the south.

The most striking feature at the rear of Banbury South (Fig. 389) is the bricked-up locking frame windows. Banbury was right in the thick of it in World War II and the locomotive depot had a corrugated iron shelter over the ash pit so that the glow from the embers of a dropped fire could not be seen at night by enemy bombers. Not far away is a supply and stores depot at Bicester, and explosives and ammunition were the staple diet of freight trains then.

Fig. 390 shows the layout of Banbury station looking towards Banbury South signal box, which can be seen just beyond the class 165 DMU. There are two sidings on the left and these are known as the 'cattle roads' – Banbury was a centre for cattle movement when such traffic went by railway until 1975. Banbury had the largest cattle market in Europe until it was abandoned in 1998. The sidings have now been converted into DMU servicing roads – *see* Fig. 387.

Then there is the up siding and up goods loop continuing through the station from Fig. 384. The DMU is standing at platform 4 and there is a train due on platform 3, as the banner repeater tells us; the repeater is for the platform starter BS2, which is a colour light signal. The semaphore signal is for platform 4.

The south end of Banbury station looking towards Banbury South signal box is shown in Fig. 391. The BS2 signal mentioned in Fig. 390 in connection with the fibre-optic repeater is on the end of the up platform. The class 66 with block train is passing the box and moving slowly along the down relief line up to signal BN4, which we saw in Fig. 386. The two home signals on the right were recently put in for the Reading rebuilding work to enable First Great Western and Chiltern trains to start from there. There had previously been ground discs there and those are not permissible for passenger trains.

Fig. 390 Banbury South track layout, November 2004.

Fig. 391 A class 66 takes the avoiding line at Banbury South, September 2014.

Colthrop Crossing

Date Built	1912
GWR Type or Builder	GWR Type 7c
No. of Levers	IFS Panel
Way of Working	Gate box
Current Status	Active
Listed (Y/N)	N

Colthrop Crossing is situated on the Berks and Hants line, which was built in competition with the London and South Western Railway. It originally ran from Reading to Devizes and was later extended to Cogload Junction near Taunton. Only the latter part survives and the line was used by crack expresses to the southwest, missing out Bristol.

Colthrop crossing is now only a gate box supervising its own crossing and that of two others at Thatcham and Midgham.

Fig. 392 shows an autumn view with winter-flowering pansies in the small window boxes. Note the white-painted rails that we first saw at Par station, the purpose of which is to lower surface temperature at perceived weak spots on the track. The box is still hanging onto its cast name plate.

Looking at Colthrop Crossing from the rear (Fig. 393), you can see the large lookout window to spot oncoming traffic. This box is controlled by Reading area signalling centre and is 48 miles and 75 chains (78.8km) from Paddington.

Fig. 392 Colthrop Crossing signal box, Berkshire, November 2005.

Fig. 393   Colthrop Crossing signal box rear view, November 2005.

Fig. 394   Greenford East signal box, London, September 2014.

Greenford East (GE)

Date Built	*c.*1904
GWR Type or Builder	GWR Type 27c
No. of Levers	76
Way of Working	TCB
Current Status	Active
Listed (Y/N)	N

Greenford was the manufacturing base of the Joe Lyons empire, which consisted of Lyons' Corner Houses and a brand of cakes and other food products to support the popular cafés and offered for retail sale. Lyons also pioneered the commercial use of computers with the Lyons Electronic Office, LEO.

Only the cakes now survive as the Kipling brand, although sold off. The site covered 63 acres (25 hectares) and was served by the GWR. The GWR had special refrigerated wagons that were used to transport some of Lyons products.

Greenford East is the last surviving GWR mechanical signal box in the London area. It is in the triangle of lines formed by the Paddington West of England main line and what is now Marylebone to Snow Hill Birmingham lines together with a chord to enable trains from Reading to access High Wycombe. The London Underground winds its way in too.

Fig. 394 is Greenford East box with signal number GE55 by the box. This signal is the down main starter towards Northolt Junction and Banbury. The bridge in the background carries the London Underground Limited (LUL) Central Line and was manufactured by the Cleveland Bridge Co. in Darlington and installed in 1939 just before the outbreak of World War II. They are still in production in Darlington.

Greenford station has two LUL platforms for the Central Line but also has a Network Rail terminus platform. Fig. 395 is the NR platform starter signal, GE29. This line dives under the Central Line

Fig. 395   Greenford East platform starter signal, April 2006.

track on the right and emerges to split, going either to West Ealing towards Paddington or Hanwell towards Reading.

South Wales

South Wales was one of the cradles of the industrial revolution in the eighteenth and nineteenth centuries. Some of the earliest examples of the iron and steel industry were to be found in the steep valleys of South Wales. The region became the largest exporter of coal in the world and Newport once held the title as the place where the most coal was exported from. Merthyr Tydfil, with the Dowlais iron works, also held the record at one time of being the largest producer of iron in the world. The very first cheque for £1 million pounds was signed at the Coal Exchange in Cardiff in 1909. The building is now the subject of an appeal for its restoration.

Tin plating was a large part of industry in South Wales and its maritime proximity to Cornwall was undoubtedly a factor in the growth of that business. This helped spawn the tinned food industry before the growth of the domestic refrigerator and freezer market.

These industries went into decline in the 1930s and new industries took their place, very largely in engineering and manufacturing.

The area and the scenery in South Wales can be very beautiful and was eulogized by William Wordsworth. Much of it that suffered the depredations of heavy industry is returning to its former attractiveness.

As not all the boxes are connected, the simplest way is to start at the far eastern end at Bishton Crossing and work westwards, going up the valleys as required. The route diagram is in Fig. 396.

Bishton Crossing

Date Built	1941
GWR Type or Builder	GWR Type 12a
No. of Levers	3
Way of Working	Gate box
Current Status	Active
Listed (Y/N)	N

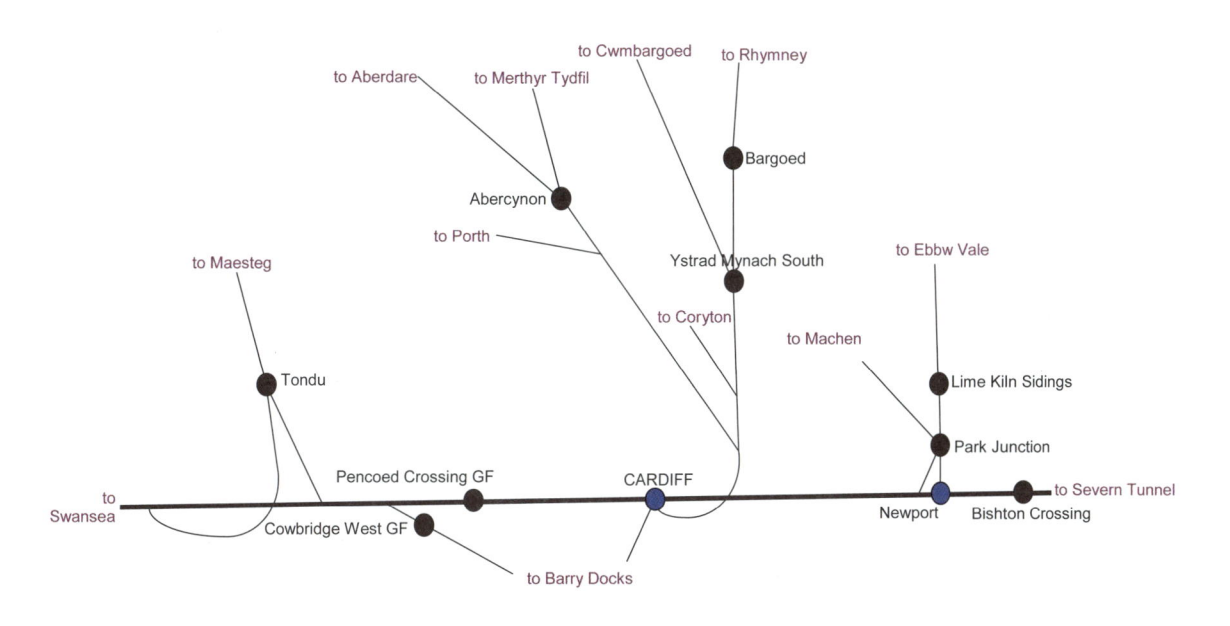

Fig. 396 South Wales diagram of signal boxes and routes.

Fig. 397　Bishton Crossing signal box, November 2009.

Fig. 398　Park Junction signal box, Newport, August 2006.

Bishton Crossing is unusual in that it spans four tracks (Fig. 397). It had been a block post up until 1961. This is the last surviving GWR gate wheel, where a signaller closes and locks gates mechanically from the box, and is a typical wartime box with the corrugated roof. The four tracks stem from Severn Tunnel Junction with associated relief lines for Llanwern steelworks, which is nearby. The four tracks then continue to Newport. The crossing continues despite a bridge over a road where the headroom under the railway is only 5ft 7in (1.7m). This means that any vehicle taller than a saloon car has to use the crossing.

Park Junction (PJ)

Date Built	1900
GWR Type or Builder	GWR Type 7b
No. of Levers	100
Way of Working	TCB, NSKT, OTS
Current Status	Active
Listed (Y/N)	N

The story of Park Junction Newport (Fig. 398) is an example of the loss of freight traffic generally on railways. At its peak there were up to six running lines outside the box and a dedicated line to the docks from here, as well as two steam loco depots with over 200 engines allocated in both Newport depots. The branch to Ebbw Vale was a hive of activity with a large engine shed and junction at Aberbeeg, about 14 miles (23km) up the valley.

The passenger traffic to Ebbw Vale has been reintroduced, however, and the layout changed to suit since the survey. For example, the 3ft freight signal arms have been replaced with 4ft passenger ones.

Lines from Cardiff and Newport meet here, after which there are branches to Machen and Ebbw Vale. Both branches are single track – the branch to Ebbw Vale starts off as double track but singles after about half a mile.

Fig. 398 depicts the five-cowl ventilator box, which is the largest remaining ex-GWR box, at 100 levers. The lines from Newport and Cardiff are worked TCB. The branch to Machen is worked one train staff, and to Ebbw Vale, no signaller key token. At the time of the survey the line to Ebbw Vale led to the disused galvanizing and tin plate works of Corus, as it then was. The last freight train ran in 2003 and that was to dispose of what was left of the works.

Fig. 399 shows the layout of incoming lines. The branches to Ebbw Vale and Machen are behind the camera. The line to Gaer Junction Newport, single track, is to the left, and the double track is towards Ebbw Junction and Cardiff, which is where the Newport main steam shed was with 140

Fig. 399   Park Junction signal box and the junction's layout, August 2006.

Fig. 400   Lime Kiln Sidings signal box, September 2006.

locomotives allocated at one time. The siding with the stop sign on it is the so-called 'Five Whistle Road' siding, where, presumably, a driver would whistle five times to alert the signaller that he wanted to go there. What is now a siding was a separate goods line to Newport docks from here. Newport Pill engine shed was at the docks. The elevated disc on the bracket signal is for Five Whistle Road.

Lime Kiln Sidings

Date Built	1887
GWR Type or Builder	GWR Type 3
No. of Levers	29
Way of Working	Gate box
Current Status	Demolished by 2008
Listed (Y/N)	N

The very name of this box is an indicator of the type of activities carried out here associated with the iron and steel industry. More recently, it was just a gate box, which was out of use at the time of the survey (Fig. 400), as the Ebbw Vale line itself was out of use. Since the restoration of passenger services in Ebbw Vale, barriers have been installed and the crossing is worked remotely by CCTV from Park Junction signal box. The box was 6 miles and 15 chains (10km) from Park Junction.

Ystrad Mynach South (YM)

Date Built	c.1885
GWR Type or Builder	Mackenzie & Holland Type 3 Rhymney Railway
No. of Levers	45
Way of Working	AB, TS&T, NSKT
Current Status	Demolished 2013
Listed (Y/N)	N

The Rhymney Railway was another of those railways absorbed by the GWR in 1923 and whose main business was the movement of coal. The box worked NSKT to Rhymney and train staff and ticket to Cwmbargoed, which is a collection of coal facilities and works and an open cast mine. The signal box, although demolished, is planned to be reconstructed elsewhere in a museum.

The box was perched on the side of an embankment (Fig. 401), and this lent a good view to either side of a curving line. There was also a small branch line to Cylla, but this had been out of use for some years. The branch to Cwmbargoed had originally been double track and passenger-carrying, and there were a further two platforms at Ystrad Mynach station to service this facility. The station that remains is just under half a mile from the site of the signal box. Ystrad Mynach had a goods loop

Fig. 401   Ystrad Mynach South signal box, September 2006.

Fig. 402   Ystrad Mynach station and signals, September 2006.

on the down side, and down in this case means towards Cardiff Queen Street station. There was also a refuge siding on the up side. The goods loop is just in front of the box. The line was double track up the Rhymney branch as far as Bargoed.

The view from the up platform but towards Cardiff Queen Street station is shown in Fig. 402. The disc and subsidiary arms on both bracket signals are to admit trains to the down goods loop, the disc via a crossover. The left-hand signal is for trains coming from Rhymney; a train is expected for Cardiff from the down platform. The bracket signal on the right is for trains coming off the Cwmbargoed branch.

Bargoed (BD)

Date Built	1970
GWR Type or Builder	BR Western Region Type 37b
No. of Levers	51
Way of Working	AB, NSKT
Current Status	Demolished 2013
Listed (Y/N)	N

Bargoed signal box was just over 4 miles (6.5km) on the double track from Ystrad Mynach. From Bargoed to Rhymney the remaining 6 miles (10km) of single track were worked with NSKT. Fig. 403 gives an overview of the station site together with the box and some signals. The box was originally

Fig. 403   Bargoed signal box and station, September 2006.

sited at Cymmer Afan, much further west towards Swansea and the Rhondda Valley. The line on the left, continuing round to the right, is the single track to Rhymney. The right-hand line is termed the 'dump siding' but was used in the days when Bargoed only had a down platform. A train would arrive from Cardiff and then had to use the dump siding while another train from Rhymney needed to access the down platform. The spur siding on the far left is for similar manoeuvrings. There is a stone-built goods shed behind the box but it has found another use now.

Abercynon (A)

Date Built	1932
GWR Type or Builder	GWR Type 27c
No. of Levers	35
Way of Working	AB, NSKT, OTS
Current Status	Demolished 2013
Listed (Y/N)	N

Abercynon signal box used to control the junction where the Taff Vale Railway lines split to go to Aberdare or Merthyr Tydfil. There were two stations, north and south for the two respective destinations. This was changed in 2008, when the two stations become one; the connections between the two lines changed and the signal box closed, although it was still in use for housing electrical equipment. It has subsequently been demolished.

The Taff Vale Railway made a junction at Pontypridd and the lines are considered down to Pontypridd and up towards Merthyr, although the mileages are calculated from Cardiff.

The box worked AB to Radyr Junction power box. The branches were worked NSKT to Merthyr Tydfil and OTS to Aberdare and Tower Colliery. Aberdare had a successful cable works and in 1939 supplied twenty-seven wagons full of mains supply cable to Norway. The cable was shipped from Newcastle-upon-Tyne.

Tower Colliery was closed as the last deep mine in South Wales in 1994 as it was considered uneconomic, but is now producing coal again. The idea occurred to someone to 'lift the lid' off and basically turn the mine into a quarry. This has made it economic again, using large earth-moving equipment.

There were estimated to be 16 million tons of coal reserves there. The mine/quarry feeds the coal-hungry Aberthaw power station. There are two trains carrying 1,500–1,600 tonnes each per day, usually class 66 hauled.

Fig. 404 shows the box in its last eighteen months of operation with almost as many windows at the rear as at the front, and the rear ones are not disfigured with the ASBO-resistant mesh grilles. Although the wooden staircase is a reproduction, some of the original windows survive and the ridge tiles are quite decorative for a box born in the Depression. The cast iron railings along the rear of the box are typical of pre-grouping railways and may well be Taff Vale Railway originals. The bracket signal behind the box carries the starters for both branches. Only the branch to Merthyr was passenger-carrying at this point. Abercynon was 16 miles and 28 chains (26.3km) from Cardiff East Junction, just by Cardiff Central station.

Fig. 405 shows the bracket signal and ground discs. The signals are for the down line towards Pontypridd and are labelled 'Down Merthyr' on the left and 'Down Aberdare' on the right. This is perhaps because there were two separate stations here, and the left is for the south station and the right for the north. The discs are to access the up goods loop.

Fig. 404 Abercynon signal box rear view, September 2006.

Fig. 405   Abercynon bracket signal, September 2006.

Pencoed Crossing Ground Frame

Date Built	c.1905
GWR Type or Builder	GWR Type 27c
No. of Levers	IFS Panel
Way of Working	Gate box
Current Status	Demolished 2007
Listed (Y/N)	N

Back on the South Wales main line now and a box living on borrowed time. It had controlled the signalling at Pencoed Station and, like so many others, found a reprieve in controlling a crossing (Fig. 406). The running lines are controlled by the Cardiff Area signalling centre and the box was 186 miles and 56 chains (300.5km) from Paddington. The internet has many references to motorists gambling with their lives to avoid waiting at the crossing for trains, resulting in some tragic incidents. The crossing is now CCTV monitored and sees 160 trains per day.

Cowbridge Road (CF)

Date Built	1965
GWR Type or Builder	BR Western Region Hut
No. of Levers	IFS Panel
Way of Working	TCB, AB
Current Status	Demolished 2013
Listed (Y/N)	N

Back on the Barry Docks loop line towards Aberthaw, Cowbridge Road (Fig. 407) was there to admit trains to the Ford engine plant at Waterston. It also controlled a crossover. It worked TCB to Port Talbot power box and AB to Aberthaw. It was 18 miles and 53 chains (30km) from Cardiff East Junction.

Fig. 406   Pencoed Crossing signal box, September 2006.

Fig. 407   Cowbridge Road signal box, September 2006.

Fig. 408 Tondu bracket signal, September 2006.

Tondu (TU)

Date Built	1884
GWR Type or Builder	GWR Type 3+
No. of Levers	65
Way of Working	AB, NSKT
Current Status	Active
Listed (Y/N)	N

Tondu signal box was another junction that was a hive of activity in the steam era, with a large junction station, goods yards and a roundhouse-type loco shed. It has survived, just. The box works AB to Port Talbot power box, Bridgend Junction, and NSKT to Port Talbot at Newlands junction. Finally, it works NSKT to Maesteg, the end of the branch line. There is also a disused branch line to Blaengarw.

Windows apart, the box has lost a lot of its original characteristics but still supervises a multiple junction with sidings and loops.

The line to Maesteg curves around to the left at the top of Fig. 408, and the rather overgrown track on the right of that is the Llynfi goods loop. Just at the beginning of that track is the disused Blaengarw branch line. The lines from the South Wales main line come in from the bottom of the picture.

Fig. 409 is the view from the platform at Tondu looking towards Maesteg, and a train is signalled for

Fig. 409 Tondu station and the route set for Maesteg, September 2006.

that branch. The right-hand signal on the bracket is for Blaengarw, and the stencil box route indicator is to differentiate between the main running line down the Blaengarw branch or the loop. The elevated disc refers to the goods loop off the Maesteg branch, the Llynfi loop referred to in Fig. 408. Note the period speed restriction signs rather than the more recent roundel type.

In Fig. 410 the token is collected at Tondu from a class 150 DMU train from Maesteg; this is an NSKT working.

Fig. 411 is the other side of the station platform, which used to form a V-shaped platform at the junction. The line goes to Margam near Port Talbot, and the loop is to enable a train at the platform to be passed by one going on to Maesteg.

177

Fig. 410 Tondu signal box token exchange off the Maesteg branch, October 2014.

Fig. 411 Tondu station and closed platform towards Margam, October 2014.

West Wales

It has always been a matter of debate where South Wales ends and west Wales begins, so the demarcation here is rather arbitrary. For our purposes, Port Talbot and anything west of there has been considered as west Wales.

Fig. 412 is a schematic representation of the tracks controlled by signalling from Port Talbot in the east to Fishguard and Milford Haven in the west. Fishguard was not only a ferry port to Ireland but before Word War I was also a port where passengers and mail could be dropped off from ocean liners on their way to Liverpool. The *Mauretania* and *Lusitania* were pre-war visitors. The *Lusitania* was torpedoed in 1915.

Swansea grew to prominence in the eighteenth century as a centre for the smelting of copper, when the city became known as 'Copperopolis'. The area grew even more with increasing coal production, and particularly high-calorific anthracite-type coals. The import of raw materials and export of finished goods saw Swansea docks grow in size to 269 acres (109 hectares) at its peak.

Port Talbot was also a port that saw prodigious growth and is now still concerned with the steel industry at nearby Margam.

The same procedure as with South Wales is adopted, in that we will start in the east and finish in the west.

Neath and Brecon Junction (NB)

Date Built	1892
GWR Type or Builder	GWR Type 5
No. of Levers	14
Way of Working	TCB, OTS
Current Status	Active
Listed (Y/N)	N

178

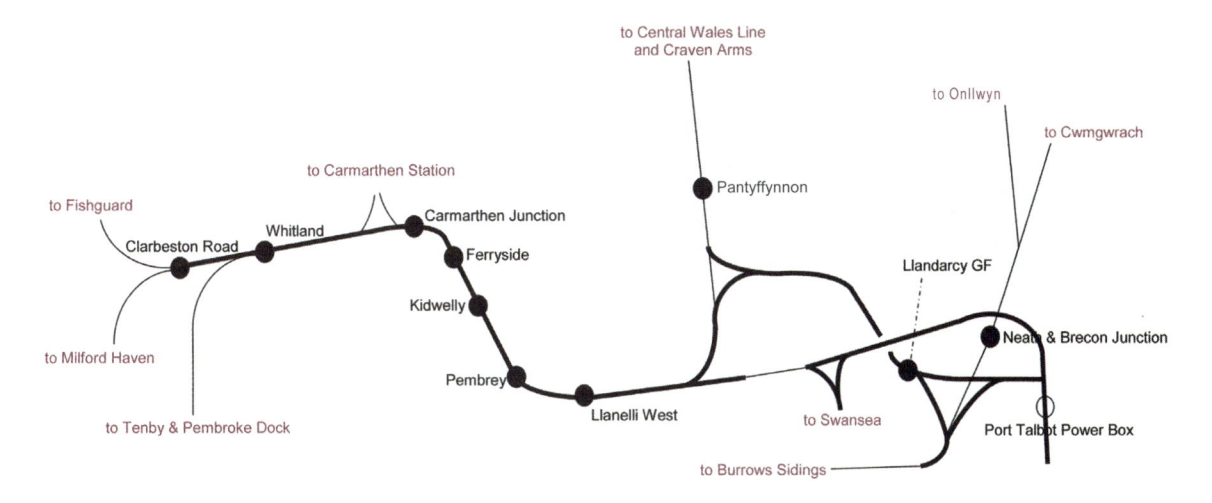

Fig. 412 West Wales layout of routes and signal boxes.

Neath and Brecon Junction was a complex junction of lines from Swansea docks, with a connection to the LNWR/LMS, to Aberdare and Crumlin High Level. The other leg of the branch was to Brecon and Talyllyn Junction. The two lines that remain go to Onllwyn coal washery and distribution centre on the one hand, and other colliery workings at Aberpergwm on the other. Class 66 locomotives work the trains to the Onllwyn Washery. Aberpergwm colliery is now a drift mine with about 7.6 million tonnes of reserves. The mine supplies top-grade anthracite, mostly to Tata steel at Port Talbot.

The box stands on the end of the platform of the long-closed Neath Riverside station. (Fig. 413). The box works OTS along both branches and TCB to Port Talbot power box. The actual junction and signals are the other side of the bridge.

Llandarcy Ground Frame

Date Built	1920
GWR Type or Builder	GWR Type 7d
No. of Levers	20
Way of Working	GF
Current Status	Closed 2013
Listed (Y/N)	N

Llandarcy ground frame had previously been Lonlas South signal box and assumed its last name in 1923; at this time it was a block post. Later it was used just to control the entry to the sidings at the BP oil refinery and so was downgraded to a ground frame. The refinery had been the first in Britain, using crude oil imported through Swansea docks, but was damaged by enemy bombing in World War II and closed in 1998.

Llandarcy was named after William Knox D'Arcy, who discovered oil in Persia (in what is now

Fig. 413 Neath and Brecon Junction signal box, October 2014.

Fig. 414   Llandarcy signal box, September 2006.

Iran) and founded the Anglo Persian Oil Company, which became BP.

Fig. 414 shows a remarkably original structure from the top up, while the lower half is considerably altered. The remains of the oil refinery are in the background. The lines in the front of the box to the left go to Court Sart Junction Neath, which joins with the South Wales main line. Court Sart was also the site of a large engine shed at Neath that had a double roundhouse. The line to the right heads west to Llanelli and Carmarthen. The line to the rear of the box is the reception loop line for oil tanker wagons arriving from Swansea docks. There was a crossover to allow trains leaving the BP complex to regain the South Wales main line towards Cardiff.

Pantyffynnon (PF)

Date Built	1892
GWR Type or Builder	GWR Type 5
No. of Levers	49
Way of Working	AB, NSTR OTS
Current Status	Active
Listed (Y/N)	Y

Heading into Carmarthenshire, Pantyffynnon is another place that has shrunk in importance and facilities over the years. The station was a multi-platformed junction with goods yards and, from 1931, a loco depot. The loco shed was built under the 1929 Loans and Guarantees Act and so resembled Didcot, which was financed under the same act of parliament. Didcot survives and is home to the Great Western Society.

Pantyffynnon is also the southern end of the Central Wales line, which, although it was LNWR/LMS in ownership, now has two ex-GWR signal boxes at either end. The other is Craven Arms, which we have met already. There is also a branch to a drift coal mine at Gwaun cae Gurwen, and class 66 locomotives motor down there with MEA open box wagons. This branch is worked OTS. The Central Wales line is worked NSTR and the section is to Llandeilo, where the train driver must exchange the token for the next section on towards Craven Arms. There are six sections on the Central Wales line in all. The box works AB to Port Talbot power box.

Fig. 415 shows Pantyffynnon signal box looking up the line towards Llanelli. The bracket signal along the line is to signal, on the left, to the Gwaun cae Gurwen branch for the coal trains. The right side is for Pantyffynnon station platform.

The siding to the right is described as the washery siding, as Gwaun cae Gurwen had a coal washery there. It was used to hold a train while a passenger train passed by on the running line. The wonky period speed restriction sign refers to the

Fig. 415   Pantyffynnon signal box, September 2006.

coal mine branch, which is about 7 miles (11km) long.

Fig. 416 shows Pantyffynnon station, looking back from the signal box and towards Llandeilo, the next token station on the Central Wales line, which is about 8 miles (13km) distant. The single-line token section starts right after the crossing at the end of the platform where the white board is.

The bracket signal would need to be seen by a train setting out from the washery siding, and the platform starter has its lever most of the way up the post to mitigate tampering. The discs cover all moves in and around the Gwaun cae Gurwen branch sidings on the right. The branch no longer needs to access the platform, as it is now freight only, but did once upon a time. The station building is now being refurbished.

Llanelli West

Date Built	c.1877
GWR Type or Builder	GWR Type 2
No. of Levers	IFS Panel
Way of Working	Gate box
Current Status	Active 2013
Listed (Y/N)	Y

Llanelli once had five signal boxes and the town was a centre for tin-plate production, steel manufacture and coal mining to the extent that Llanelli was known as 'Tinopolis'. The maritime proximity to the tin mines of Cornwall provided ready material. Llanelli also had extensive goods yards, a large locomotive depot and a splendid station in characterful stone, which has survived. The same group that were responsible for listing the goods shed were active in securing the listing for the signal box with CADW, the Welsh heritage organization. Listing usually means that a building will continue in its function for longer, as the building has to be maintained anyway.

Fig. 417 shows the fourth oldest signal box in Wales in fine condition, although its function has been reduced to that of gate box in a TCB colour light signal area. There is an individual function switch

Fig. 416 Pantyffynnon station and yard area, September 2006.

Fig. 417 Llanelli West ground frame signal box, March 2006.

(IFS) panel in the box together with CCTV monitors for adjacent crossings. There are two crossings, one at each end of the station platforms. Llanelli West ground frame is 225 miles and 28 chains (362.7km) from Paddington via Stroud in Gloucestershire.

Pembrey (PY)

Date Built	1907
GWR Type or Builder	GWR Type 7+
No. of Levers	83
Way of Working	AB
Current Status	Active
Listed (Y/N)	N

Fig. 418   Pembrey signal box, March 2006.

Fig. 419   Kidwelly signal box, October 2014.

Pembrey is the signal box for Pembrey and Burry Port station, which is just over half a mile away to the west of the box. The Burry Port and Gwendraeth Valley Railway was established in 1859 to service a number of collieries up the valley, and later developed passenger traffic. The line was notable for two things. Firstly, it had a number of low bridges that restricted the height and width of locomotives and rolling stock using the line. Locomotives had to be specially built or adapted and later on in the line's life the GWR built special coaches for it. The second notable feature was that Colonel Holman Fred Stephens got involved with the line at one point. Col. Stephens was based in Kent and took on many ailing railway concerns; among the many were the Shropshire and Montgomeryshire Light Railway, whose base was at Shrewsbury; the Weston Clevedon and Portishead Railway; and the Ffestiniog Railway.

What was not unusual was that the clerk drafting the act of parliament for the railway in the mid-nineteenth century was not entirely conversant with place name spelling in Wales and spelled the name wrong on the act – it should be Gwendreath. There was a further branch line from Kidwelly a little way up the line and it was this that survived until recent times.

With the tendency to unstaffed stations nowadays, it is refreshing to see a business called the Ticket Hut operating a service for passengers on the station.

Fig. 418 shows a signal box on steroids compared with the job it now has to do. There are no sidings or points to control, only signals and a crossing. At least it is an absolute block post, however. From Paddington to Llanelli the line is TCB and from here on it is AB. The box has been rebuilt twice, as it was damaged by train derailments in 1912 and 1964. It only had thirty-one levers when it started off in life in 1907. The current lever frame dates to 1953.

Kidwelly (K)

Date Built	1885
GWR Type or Builder	Hybrid GWR and BR WR Type 35
No. of Levers	IFS Panel
Way of Working	AB
Current Status	Active
Listed (Y/N)	N

Kidwelly is the signal box for the last remaining branch of the Burry Port and Gwendraeth Valley

Railway; although the branch line was lifted in 2005, some of the loop and sidings connected with the branch remain. Some track also remains at Pontyates, further up the line.

Fig. 419 shows the box, which has a curious past. It started off life in 1885 as a GWR-built unit and had its top replaced in the 1950s, and its frame replaced by an IFS panel. The remains of the Burry Port and Gwendraeth Valley Railway are to the left and on the same side of the tracks as the camera.

Ferryside (F)

Date Built	1880s
GWR Type or Builder	GWR Type 3
No. of Levers	24
Way of Working	AB
Current Status	Active
Listed (Y/N)	N

Ferryside signal box has a delightful location on the estuary of the River Towy. It has fine sandy beaches, and was once on the route to Llanstephan Castle across the estuary, hence the need for the ferry. It also has an ancient church, St Ishmael's.

It developed into a fishing port and in recent years played a part in the cockling industry, seeing some conflict between rival cockling gangs, but is now mostly popular with retired people. The station is only a request stop – a prospective passenger at the station has to use hand signals to the train driver, but the signaller could intervene.

There is a trailing crossover here as well as a road crossing.

Fig. 420 shows the box on the station platform together with home signals and the crossing. The single point rodding for the trailing crossover can be seen running along the trackside below the down platform. The line curves away to the left to follow the estuary, and the beach is just beyond the station to the right. Llanstephan Castle is on the opposite bank of the estuary.

Carmarthen Junction (CJ)

Date Built	1956
GWR Type or Builder	BR WR Type 16a
No. of Levers	OCS Panel
Way of Working	AB, TCB
Current Status	Active
Listed (Y/N)	N

Carmarthen Junction used to be the junction for the line through Carmarthen station to Aberystwyth via Strata Florida, but the line terminates at the station now. The junction is formed by the main line as it continues past the box further into west Wales.

Carmarthen is the county town and an administrative centre on the river. In earlier times the town was divided by the River Towy into two

Fig. 420 Ferryside signal box, March 2006.

Fig. 421 Carmarthen Junction signal box, October 2014.

communities that were not united until 1546. Carmarthen then enjoyed considerable importance and prestige. The economic centre of gravity shifted towards Swansea in the nineteenth century with its steel and coal mining industries. Carmarthen remains a delightful town, still dominated by the river and occasionally humbled by it.

Carmarthen Junction signal box in shown in Fig. 421 and is reminiscent of the Festival of Britain style of Kidderminster. The box is equipped with a one control switch panel (OCS). This enables a signaller to set up a route with one switch but there are other switches that can vary that one switch setting. Consequently there are no mechanical signals or points at this box.

Carmarthen Junction works AB to Ferryside and TCB to Whitland. The signal box is 245 miles and 10 chains (394.5km) from Paddington via Stroud.

Whitland (W)

Date Built	1972
GWR Type or Builder	BR WR Type 37b
No. of Levers	39
Way of Working	TCB
Current Status	Active
Listed (Y/N)	N

Whitland is not named a junction but is one. The line splits here into the main line west and the branch to Pembroke Dock. The latter has the pretty resort of Tenby on its route and this attracts an HST service down the branch on summer Saturdays. Both Tenby and Pembroke Dock have fine stations in local stone.

Going back to the first millennium, Whitland was named the first Welsh parliament. It was also home to a Cistercian abbey that is now a ruin.

Whitland was a further junction for Cardigan. This meandering branch line was fairly laid back in that it took a train one hour forty minutes to cover the 14½ miles (23km) from Whitland to Cardigan, with nine intermediate stops. The branch closed completely in 1963.

Whitland had its own loco shed and goods yard, and, as it was the focal point for rural life, had a considerable dairy industry locally. Until the 1950s the Whitland–Kensington Olympia milk train was a regular runner. The train was limited to 505 tonnes, which was seventeen milk tankers and a van. Each milk tank was capable of holding 3,000 gallons (13,620 litres) of milk. The Whitland dairy closed finally in 2014.

Fig. 422 shows Whitland signal box is in the style of Evesham, though perhaps with even less flair. The station is behind the camera, complete with a bay platform and sidings. The footbridge has a cast iron plate announcing Horsehay 1934. This was a famous firm of bridge builders situated off the Lightmoor Junction/Madeley branch in Shropshire.

Fig. 422 Whitland signal box, October 2014.

Clarbeston Road (CR)

Date Built	1906
GWR Type or Builder	GWR Type 7c
No. of Levers	OCS Panel
Way of Working	TCB
Current Status	Active
Listed (Y/N)	N

We finish in the beautiful county of Pembrokeshire at the final junction for Fishguard and Milford Haven.

Fishguard had been carved and blasted out by the GWR from solid rock and so any expansion would have been tricky. It is still a ferry port though the ocean liner traffic eventually moved from Liverpool to Southampton in the 1930s.

Almost by compensation, the deep-water port of Milford Haven had been thought of as an anchorage for the entire Royal Navy fleet but was eventually developed into a supertanker base for crude oil and liquid petroleum gas imports. It remains so today.

Another generator of traffic past the box and junction was the Royal Naval Armaments Depot at Trecwn on the Fishguard line. This was open until 1998 and was a store for mines, shells and explosives. There was a 2ft 6in gauge narrow gauge railway where much of the fittings were of copper to minimize the risk of explosions. Some of the RNAD narrow gauge locos and rolling stock has found its way onto preserved narrow gauge lines. Much of the original standard gauge interface to the depot is still there.

Clarbeston Road (Fig. 423) is still deep in TCB territory so there are no mechanical signals or rod-operated points. Still, it is an interesting box architecturally, if not operationally. Note the curious middle window arrangement and the token-catcher apparatus to the left of the box. This would have had a white-painted net within the square metal frame. The token would have been contained in a pouch with a hoop on it to lasso the arm sticking out.

Gloucestershire, Somerset and Avon

The fact that these three counties have been lumped together is an indication of how the mechanical signalling picture looks there. There is only one box that still has rodding and signal wires coming out of it.

Moreton-in-Marsh is in Gloucestershire but has already been covered on the Cotswold Line section. Also in Gloucestershire we have Awre, Lydney Crossing ground frame and St Mary's crossing. In Somerset there is Yeovil Pen Mill, together with Puxton and Worle Crossing, while in Avon there is only St Andrew's Junction.

Awre

Date Built	1909
GWR Type or Builder	GWR Type 7d+
No. of Levers	–
Way of Working	–
Current Status	Closed
Listed (Y/N)	N

We head into Gloucestershire on the Gloucester–Newport line. Unlikely as it seems when you look at the site today, Awre was a junction with the Forest of Dean Central Railway, later taken over by the GWR. The Forest of Dean was a considerable producer of coal until the 1960s and still has some mines left working. The miners have been granted an old right as Freeminers, as a privilege for residing in a certain part of the Forest of Dean.

Fig. 423 Clarbeston Road signal box, October 2014.

Fig. 424   Awre signal box, September 2006.

The line ran to collieries at Blakeney and Howbeach Sidings. It was eventually closed in 1959. The last revenue-earning trip on the line had been ten years earlier.

The box last saw service in 1973 as a gate box for the crossing but that function has been taken over using CCTV at Lydney. The box in Fig. 424 looks neglected and has been used as a store for some years. It is substantially original except for the windows.

Lydney Crossing Ground Frame

Date Built	*c.*1918
GWR Type or Builder	GWR Type 27c
No. of Levers	IFS Panel
Way of Working	Gate box
Current Status	Demolished Dec. 2012
Listed (Y/N)	N

Still on the Gloucester–Newport line, we move to the junction of the Forest of Dean Railways with the main line. There was a plethora of lines and goods yards, some going down to Lydney docks, from the Forest of Dean and its collieries. The present Dean Forest preservation line has a station at Lydney Junction at right angles to the GWR main-line station of Lydney and there are still a number of sidings and loops present, but none operated by Lydney Crossing ground frame.

Lydney Crossing GF was in later years simply a gate box supervising a busy road crossing. It also, after 1973, monitored Awre by CCTV. Fig. 425 presents a mostly wooden box with a curious brick-built rebuild of one end and the door to the stairs round the front instead of the side. Inevitably the windows have changed but much else is original.

Fig. 426 shows how you support a box that has the River Lyd nearby with a steep bank down to it.

Fig. 425   Lydney Crossing Ground Frame signal box, November 2003.

Fig. 426   Lydney Crossing Ground Frame signal box rear view, suspended, November 2003.

The brick pillars are doing useful work in stopping the rot to the timber sides nearest the floor.

The box was demolished and control of its crossings passed to Cardiff.

St Mary's Crossing

Date Built	c.1870
GWR Type or Builder	GWR Type 2
No. of Levers	–
Way of Working	Gate box
Current Status	Active
Listed (Y/N)	Y

Gloucestershire also has the line from Swindon to Gloucester running through it through Stroud.

St Mary's Crossing has been just that since it was built, although originally it did control some signals to guard the crossing and there was a halt there until 1964. The area is now controlled from Gloucester but local operation of the crossing remains.

Not far away is Brimscombe station, where there was a loco shed to house the engines that banked mostly freight trains up the fearsome gradients in and around the Sapperton Tunnels.

Fig. 427 is of St Mary's Crossing signal box in the beautiful Golden Valley south of Stroud. Stroud still has a Brunel stone goods shed.

Yeovil Pen Mill

Date Built	1937
GWR Type or Builder	GWR Type 11+
No. of Levers	65
Way of Working	AB, KT, NSKT
Current Status	Active
Listed (Y/N)	N

This is Somerset's only GWR mechanical signal box and it is important to realize that the preserved scene in Somerset has much more than remains on Network Rail. Yeovil is the site of Westland helicopters, now associated with an Italian company but still a major employer in the area.

Yeovil Pen Mill is on the ex-GWR route to Weymouth from Castle Cary and it has a junction with Yeovil Junction, the ex-Southern Railway station. Yeovil Pen Mill has been part of the Southern Region of Network Rail so there are some Southern Region signals to be seen. Between the junction of GWR and SR lines was a small loco depot that closed in the 1960s.

Fig. 428 shows the Yeovil Pen Mill signal box apparently suffering from the greenhouse effect with some whitewashed windows. The running lines either side of the box are flat-bottomed rail but the loop sidings are all bullhead. Note the sole lower quadrant signal.

Fig. 427 St Mary's Crossing signal box, September 2006.

Fig. 428   Yeovil Pen Mill signal box, March 2009.

Yeovil Pen Mill station (Fig. 429) has the unusual feature of having platforms on both sides of one track. This is sometimes done when a lot of people need to be de-trained quickly, for example at holiday resorts – Scarborough in North Yorkshire has two platforms like this. In the case of Pen Mill, it was perhaps to handle workers for the Westland factory, though it seems unlikely as some passengers would need to use the footbridge to exit the station.

Further along the platform there are two Southern Region bracket signals with Western Region finials, the one on the left obscured by the platform canopy. The one on the right used to be a cash register style when there were three roads to choose from. The selections were to Dorchester; to the loco shed; or to Yeovil Junction. As the loco shed is no longer with us the cash register is not needed. The only surviving Network Rail cash register now is at Worcester Shrub Hill, although there are examples on the Severn Valley Railway.

There is a sign in front of each bracket which reads 'Commencement of Token section'. The box works AB to Westbury, key token to Yeovil Junction and NSKT to Dorchester West.

Puxton and Worle Crossing

Date Built	1916
GWR Type or Builder	GWR Type 7
No. of Levers	IFS Panel
Way of Working	Gate box
Current Status	Active
Listed (Y/N)	N

Puxton and Worle Crossing is on the Bristol–Taunton line on the Bristol side of the junction with

Fig. 429   Yeovil Pen Mill station and bracket signals, March 2009.

the line to Weston-super-Mare. Puxton originally had a London Cooperative Dairy factory and trains of milk were dispatched from here.

Fig. 430 shows that Puxton and Worle is an ex-GWR box all right but has been heavily modified over the years. One curious feature is that in the days before mobile phones, or indeed telephones at all, the signaller would indicate to either the signal technician or telegraph lineman that either or both their presence was required by hanging a diamond-shaped metal plate with the letter S or T on it. If you look at the box, there is the unmistakable image of that diamond to the right-hand side, although they have not been used for maybe fifty years.

St Andrew's Junction

Date Built	1910
GWR Type or Builder	GWR Type 27c
No. of Levers	OCS and Nx Panel
Way of Working	TCB
Current Status	Active
Listed (Y/N)	N

Bristol Temple Meads station had been modernized with colour light signals in the 1930s so perhaps it is not surprising to find so little evidence of mechanical signalling or its infrastructure here.

St Andrew's Junction is in the middle of the lines around Avonmouth and Portbury Docks. Among other things, the latter lands cargoes of coal for Rugeley power station and we have seen trains from Portbury Docks at Craven Arms and Shrewsbury. They also handle other minerals and bulk cargoes. There are several sets of privately owned sidings and facilities nearby. All the traffic up to the crossing close by the box is controlled by Bristol Area Signalling Centre and all after the crossing, including the branch to Severn Beach station, by St Andrew's Junction.

St Andrew's Junction signal box is depicted in Fig. 431, though the view is obscured by the massive stop blocks at the end of the siding in front of the box. It seems likely that a bit of over-enthusiastic shunting in the past reduced the crossing gates to matchwood hence the upgraded buffer stops.

The painted numbers on the buffer stops refer to the mileages from places and the fact that the place they are calculated from changes here. It is 16 miles (26km) to Bristol Temple Meads via Pilning (Low Level) and Severn Beach, and 9 miles and 30 chains (15.1km) the other way via Clifton Down. The places mentioned don't all exist any more – it is just how it was calculated back in the day.

Fig. 430 Puxton and Worle crossing signal box, March 2009.

Fig. 431 St Andrew's Junction signal box, March 2009.

Useful Resources

Books and Written Works

Allan, I., *British Railways Pre-Grouping Atlas and Gazetteer*
Great Western Railway Magazine 1933, 1938–39
Quail Track Diagrams, Parts 3 and 4 (TrackMaps)
Signalling Record Society, *Signalling Atlas and Signal Box Directory*
Signalling Record Society, *The Signal Box Register Vol. 1 – GWR*
The works of Adrian Vaughan – various publishers

Websites

Adrian the Rock's signalling pages – www.roscalen.com/signals
The Signalbox by John Hinson – www.signalbox.org
Danny Scroggins – http://photos.signallingnotices.org.uk
2D53 by Dave Plimmer – www.2d53.co.uk/signalling

Index

Abbey Foregate 71, 72, 74–77, 128
Abercynon 171, 175, 176
Aberdare 171, 175, 179
Abergavenny 95, 99, 100, 101, 104
Abermule 48
Aberthaw 164, 175, 176
Aberystwyth 71, 159, 160, 183
Absolute Block 43, 44, 45, 48, 52, 64, 65, 66, 134, 159, 182
Ascott under Wychwood 61, 64–66
Automatic Warning System or AWS 42, 95
Awre 185, 186

Backing signal 14
Backlight blinder 16, 17, 29
Banbury 51, 79, 165–170
Bargoed 171, 174
Barr's Court 93, 94
Barry 163, 164, 171, 176
Bearley West Junction 103, 105–107
Bellcrank 10, 17, 24, 37, 38
Bell Code 46, 59, 72
Bentley Heath Crossing 103–105, 125, 153
Berth Track Circuit 41
Bewdley 14, 88, 89, 117, 156
Bidston 134, 136
Birmingham 5, 17, 20, 26, 34, 51, 52, 54, 57, 87, 103, 104, 106, 107, 110, 112–114, 117–119, 121–124, 165, 170
Bishop's Castle 82, 83
Bishton Crossing 171, 172
Blakeney 186
Bodmin and Wenford 139
Bracket signal 12, 13, 16–21, 26, 35, 36, 77, 84, 88, 89, 93, 97, 98, 100, 114, 115, 119, 127, 128, 138, 140, 144, 149, 151, 155, 156, 167, 173–177, 180, 181, 188
Bridgend 164, 177
Bridgnorth 14, 16, 118, 121
Bristol 51, 52, 72, 79, 84, 112, 169, 188, 189
British Railways or BR 9, 12, 34, 61, 62, 86, 91, 105, 118, 124, 127, 130, 146, 147, 158, 161, 174, 176, 182–184
Bromfield 34, 35, 78, 87, 88
Bromsgrove 34, 113
Brymbo 134
Burngullow-Probus 143
Burry Port and Gwendraeth Valley Railway 182, 183

Caersws 160–162
Cambrian 11, 12, 18, 30, 49, 51, 71, 72, 77, 78, 131, 159–162
Calling on 13, 14, 23, 24, 26, 53, 69, 100, 101
Camborne 153–156
Cardiff 78, 163, 171, 172, 174–176, 180, 187
Carmarthen 179, 180, 183, 184
Cash register 14, 20, 21, 120, 188
Castle Cary 21, 187
Catch Point 39, 114, 119, 123, 127, 143

Central Wales line 31, 48, 81, 83–85, 99, 179–181
Charlbury 65
Chester 5, 13, 15, 19, 20, 22, 23, 25, 51, 71, 73, 74, 84, 124, 126, 131, 132, 134–136
Chiltern Trains 122, 166–168
China clay 136, 139–142, 144–149, 151
Church Stretton 78, 80, 81, 83, 87
Churchill and Blakedown 113, 120, 121
Clarbeston Road 179, 185
Class 08 146, 147
Class 37 77
Class 43 HST 61, 144, 159, 184
Class 47 73, 166
Class 60 94, 95
Class 66 6, 84, 144, 168, 169, 175, 179, 180
Class 67 144, 145
Class 139 123, 124
Class 150 69, 110, 115, 122, 138, 149, 152, 155, 177
Class 158 77, 78, 100, 101, 133, 162
Class 166 61
Class 170 69
Class 172 115, 124
Class 175 25, 77, 78, 84, 85, 97
Class 180 61
Class 220 Voyager 144, 159
Clearing Point 46
Codsall 124–126, 129, 130
Colthrop 165, 169
Colwall 68, 70
Cornish Riviera Express 155
Cosford 124, 126–130
Cowbridge Road 176
Craven Arms 6, 14, 22, 25, 26, 29, 31, 48, 78, 83–87, 99, 125, 179, 180, 189
Crewe Junction 9, 13, 15–17, 19, 27, 71, 73, 74
Criccieth 160, 162
Croes Newydd North Fork 133–135
Cwmbargoed 171, 173, 174

Dean Forest Railway 124
Detection 14, 38
Detonator 48, 50, 84, 85
Didcot 121, 180
Distant Signal 11–13, 17, 31, 41, 50, 55, 74, 75, 134, 149, 150, 160
Doll or Dolly 15, 17, 20, 77, 98
Dorchester 188
Dorrington 77–81, 83, 132, 165
Dovey Junction 161, 162
Droitwich Spa 18, 34, 35, 46, 51, 52, 54, 55, 112–119, 143
Dutton 161, 162

Ebbw Vale 32, 34, 95, 171–173
English Bridge Junction 83, 90, 91
English Heritage 50, 82, 118
European Rail Traffic Management System or ERTMS 49, 77, 159, 161
Evans O'Donnell 164

Evesham 24, 25, 57–59, 61–64, 184
EWS 147, 149, 152, 164

Facing point 36–38, 50, 56, 84, 123, 137, 143, 144, 150, 156
Falmouth 136, 151, 152
Ferryside 179, 183, 184
First Great Western 167
Fowey 136, 139–142

Gantry, Gantries 16, 19, 20, 27, 72, 74, 75, 137
Gloucestershire and Warwickshire Railway 61, 108
Gobowen 22, 23, 27, 28, 51, 124, 131–134
Goonbarrow Junction 48, 49, 136, 142, 145, 146, 148–151
Great Malvern 68, 69
Great Western Society 180
Greenford 10, 165, 170
Ground Disc 13–16, 35, 38, 39, 74, 75, 79, 81, 94, 96, 97, 110, 119, 137, 140, 156, 168, 175
Ground frame 10, 32, 52, 53, 123, 131, 137, 160, 162, 163, 176, 179, 181, 185, 186
GSM-R 40, 49
Gwaun cae Gurwen 180, 181

Hartlebury 113, 116, 117, 118
Hatton Junction 103, 106, 107
Henley in Arden 103, 107–109
Hereford 5, 11, 12, 16–18, 20, 22, 25, 26, 30, 38, 49, 51, 52, 54, 56, 59–61, 66, 67, 70–72, 76–78, 81–85, 89–99, 101, 111, 165
Herefordshire 70, 78, 90, 93, 95
Home Signal 9, 11–13, 22, 23, 25, 26, 28, 29, 31, 32, 34, 35, 41, 50, 56, 60, 69, 70, 77, 84, 97, 98, 106, 107, 111, 112, 115, 116, 119, 120, 134, 137, 138, 156, 160–162, 166–168, 183

Individual Function Switches or IFS 86, 116, 121, 153, 154, 169, 176, 181–183, 186, 188
Intermediate Block Section or IBS 46, 144

Jellicoe Specials 78, 101

Kay's of Worcester 46
Key Token or KT 48, 49, 57, 58, 61, 63, 64, 128–131, 137, 145, 148, 150, 172–175, 177, 178, 188
Kidderminster 4, 20, 35, 71, 77, 112–123, 136, 152, 184
Kidwelly 179, 182

Lamp status 30, 31
Leamington Spa 103, 105, 106, 165–167
LED 14, 20, 27, 132, 138
Ledbury 67, 68, 70, 71, 94

191

INDEX

Leominster 29, 35, 78, 90–92
Lightmoor Junction 124, 129, 130, 184
Liskeard 25, 26, 51, 136–140
Little Mill Junction 95, 99, 101, 102
Llandarcy Ground Frame 179
Llanelli 179–182
Llanwern 6, 94, 95, 122, 172
Loans and Guarantees Act 180
London Midland Region 12, 62, 79, 105, 106, 119, 122, 124, 128, 166
London North Eastern Railway or LNER 55, 79, 134–136, 165
London North Western Railway LNWR 71–74, 78, 79, 83, 93, 99, 101, 103, 179, 180
London South Western Railway 169
Looe 136, 137, 138
Lostwithiel 136, 137, 139–144
Lower quadrant 8, 12, 13, 17, 25, 72, 79, 106, 107, 111, 126, 132, 139, 162, 166, 167, 187
Ludlow 34, 35, 37, 38, 86–89
Lydney Crossing 185, 186

Machynlleth 77, 159–162
MacKenzie and Holland 52, 59, 70, 97, 116, 117, 131
Madeley Junction 124, 128–131
Maes Level Crossing 160, 162
Maesteg 4, 171, 177, 178
Malvern Wells 67–70, 143
Marshbrook 78, 82, 83, 85
Merthyr Tydfil 99, 171, 175
Midland Railway 8, 52, 55, 57, 62, 93, 103, 113
Milford Haven 178, 185
Moreton-in-Marsh 15, 61–65, 185
Moreton on Lugg 78, 84, 88, 91–93, 111
Motorail 34, 158

National Railway Museum 8, 65
Neath and Brecon Junction 178, 179
Neath Riverside 179
Network Rail 5, 7, 9, 10, 20, 21, 23, 34, 42, 44, 47, 50
Newquay 49, 51, 136, 142–146, 148–151, 155
Newland East 59, 61, 66–68
Newport (Gwent) 5, 18, 19, 32, 35, 41, 51, 94, 95, 97, 98, 101, 171–173, 185, 186
No Signaller Key Token or NSKT 48, 137, 172–175, 177, 187, 188
No Signaller Key Token Remote or NSKTR or NSTR 48, 83
North Ground Frame 131
Northolt Junction 170
Norton Junction 43, 44, 51–53, 57, 61, 62
NX Panel 102, 189

One Train Staff or OTS 48, 121, 123, 137, 139, 145, 148, 150, 151, 175, 178, 179, 180
One Control Switch Panel or OCS 183, 184, 185, 189
Onibury 78, 83, 85–87
Oswestry 27, 131–133
Over Junction 70, 71
Oxfordshire 51, 65, 79, 165

Paddington 21, 57, 121, 125, 139, 142, 149–152, 154, 159, 169–171, 176, 181, 182, 184
Pantyffynnon 179, 180
Par 15, 16, 46, 136, 140–148, 150, 152, 155, 156
Park Junction 18, 19, 32, 35, 41, 95, 171–173
Parry Peoplemover 122, 124
Pembrey 179, 181, 182
Pembroke Dock 179, 184
Pencoed Crossing 176
Penzance 25, 51, 136, 139–142, 152, 155, 157–159
Pershore 61, 62
Pontrilas 95, 97–99, 101
Pontyates 183
Pontypool Road 101
Pontypridd 175
Port Talbot 122, 176–180
Portbury Dock 52, 72, 84, 189
Puxton and Worle 185, 188, 189
Pwllheli West Frame 160, 162, 163

Radio Electronic Tokenless Block RETB 77, 159, 161, 162
Reading 8, 46, 167–171
Rhymney 171, 174, 175
Roskear Junction 136, 152–154
Route indicator 14, 20, 21, 72, 74, 75, 124, 177
Royal Mail 27, 74
Royal Naval Armaments Depot at Trecwn 185
Royal Ordnance Factory at Glascoed 101
Rugeley 52, 72, 189

St Andrew's 112, 185, 189
St Austell 142, 151
St Blazey 48, 136, 142, 145–150
St Erth 136, 153–156, 159
St Ives 136, 148, 154–157
St Mary's 185, 187
Semaphore Signal 7, 9, 10, 20, 47, 51, 61, 66, 86, 134, 159, 165–168
Severn Bridge Junction 7, 12, 16, 30, 71–73, 75, 77, 83, 84
Severn Tunnel 78, 79, 171, 172
Severn Valley Railway or SVR 4, 14, 16, 20, 36, 77, 89, 113, 116, 118, 119–121, 136, 152, 156, 188
Shirley 103, 109, 110
Shrewsbury 5, 7, 9, 10, 12–14, 16–20, 23, 25, 27, 30, 31, 35–38, 51, 71–73, 81–85, 87–95, 101, 118, 124–126, 128, 129, 131–136, 159–161, 165, 166, 182
Shrewsbury and Chester Railway 131, 135, 136
Sighting 11, 18, 19, 24–27, 32, 34, 56, 98, 106, 152
Single Line 18, 19, 38, 43, 47–49, 57, 58, 62–64, 68, 77, 83, 85, 86, 128, 129, 136, 159, 181
Smethwick 122
Snow Hill 110, 122, 124, 125, 165, 170
Southern Railway 65, 187
SPAD or Signal Passed at Danger 10, 42
Spectacle 8, 17
Stencil box 13, 177

Stoke Junction 114
Stourbridge Junction 113, 121–124, 152
Strata Florida 183
Stratford upon Avon 61, 103, 106, 110
Stroud 120, 181, 184, 187
Sutton Bridge Junction 12–14, 18, 30, 35, 36, 71, 72, 75–80, 153, 159, 161, 162
Swansea 31, 81, 99, 164, 171, 175, 178–180, 184

Tata steel 122, 179
Telford Steam Railway 130
Tenby 179, 184
Tokenless Block or TB 49, 68, 70, 77, 93, 94, 159, 161, 162
Tondu 4, 171, 177, 178
Track circuit 39–41, 46, 54–56, 59, 64, 74, 101, 110, 126, 143, 149
Track Circuit Block or TCB 46–48, 52, 54, 55, 57, 65, 66, 74, 91–93, 99, 101, 111–113, 119, 121, 128, 133, 134, 164–167, 170, 172, 176, 178, 179, 181–185, 189
Track Circuit Operating Device or TCOD 47
Trailing point 37–39, 150
Train Out of Section 45, 46, 84
Train Register 46, 59, 72
Tram Inn 94–96
Trap Point 38, 39, 53, 63, 64, 74, 77, 127, 140, 142, 144, 146, 152
Train Protection and Warning System or TPWS 42, 107, 117
Train Staff and Ticket or TS&T 49, 173
Truro 136, 142, 150–153, 155
Tyseley 103, 106, 111, 112
Tyseley Warwick Road 112

Uninterruptible Power Supplies or UPS 22, 31
Upper quadrant 12–14, 79, 106, 107, 111, 119, 120, 126, 132, 166

Wellington (Shropshire) 18, 72–74, 128, 130
Welwyn 55, 59, 153
Westbury (Shropshire) 72
Western Region 9, 12, 52, 61, 62, 79, 119, 122, 125, 130, 151, 174, 176, 188
Whitland 179, 184
Wolverhampton 5, 17–19, 51, 52, 71, 72, 124, 125, 128, 132, 136
Woofferton Junction 16, 17, 35–39, 78, 88–90, 101
Worcester Foregate 17–19, 29, 51, 54
Worcester Shrub Hill 8, 10, 11, 15, 17, 18, 20, 21, 23, 24, 26, 32–35, 43, 44, 51–53, 57, 188
Worcestershire 52, 63, 93, 108, 112, 117
World War 52, 63, 78, 91, 101, 109, 111, 113, 116, 126, 165, 168, 170, 179
Wrexham General 42, 120, 122, 134–136

Yeovil Junction 187, 188
Yeovil Pen Mill 20, 21, 51, 185, 187, 188
Ystrad Mynach South 171, 173, 174